THE HEART
OF THE MIND

ALSO BY RUSSELL TARG AND JANE KATRA

*Miracles of Mind: Exploring Nonlocal Consciousness
and Spiritual Healing*

OTHER BOOKS COAUTHORED BY RUSSELL TARG:

Mind Reach: Scientists Look at Psychic Abilities
by Russell Targ & Harold Puthoff
Mind Race: Understanding and Using Psychic Abilities
by Russell Targ & Keith Harary
*Mind at Large: Institute of Electrical and Electronics Engineers
Symposium on the Nature of Extrasensory Perception*
edited by Charles Tart, Harold Puthoff, & Russell Targ

THE HEART
OF THE MIND

HOW TO EXPERIENCE GOD
WITHOUT BELIEF

JANE KATRA, Ph.D., & RUSSELL TARG

FOREWORD BY MARIANNE WILLIAMSON

NEW WORLD LIBRARY
NOVATO, CALIFORNIA

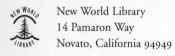

New World Library
14 Pamaron Way
Novato, California 94949

Copyright © 1999 by Jane Katra, Ph.D., and Russell Targ

Cover design: Big Fish
Cover illustration: Photonica
Text design and layout: Mary Ann Casler

Library of Congress Cataloging-in-Publication Data
Katra, Jane.
        The heart of the mind : how to experience God without belief / by Jane Katra
         & Russell Targ.
            p.   cm.
        Includes bibliographical references and index.
        ISBN 1-57731-041-1 (hardcover : alk. paper)
        ISBN 1-57731-156-6 (paperback : alk. paper)
          1. Parapsychology — Religious aspects.   2. Experience (Religion)
I. Targ, Russell. II. Title.
BL65.P3T37   1999
291.4'2—dc21   98-53427
                                                               CIP

First paperback printing, January 2000
ISBN 1-57731-156-6
Printed in Canada on acid-free, recycled paper
Distributed to the trade by Publishers Group West

10 9 8 7 6 5 4 3 2 1

For Gangaji,
with love and gratitude

Contents

The Goal

*May everyone be happy and safe, and
may their hearts be filled with joy.*

— The Buddha's teaching on love,
joy, equanimity, and compassion

The Path

*The true value of a human being is
determined primarily by the measure
and the sense in which he has
attained liberation from the self.*

— Albert Einstein

Foreword

For ages, there has been an esoteric prophecy: that in a great historical climax to come, science and religion would unite in exaltation of one great Truth.

As we approach the millennium, in every area of human endeavor, there is indeed interest in a very general concern. Whether the conversation turns to relationships, medicine, spirituality, business, science, or anything else, there is at least a faint hint of an eternal message making its way into consciousness: underlying oneness, spirit, and love.

Jane Katra and Russell Targ have looked at two specific areas — science and spirituality — with the cold eye of the scientist and the warm heart of the mystic. They have applied tough-minded scientific observation to the realms of spirit, laying out for the most rationalistic thinker some profound musings on issues of faith. In this exciting new book, Katra and Targ posit spirituality as a new scientific frontier. Applying the most disciplined investigative techniques, scientists throughout the world have now made clear that we need no longer treat faith as blind; it has revealed itself, at last, to regions of the mind formerly unable to grasp its implications. Katra and Targ have helped to unlock the long-locked door between the rooms of science and the rooms of God.

Like a great pyramid as it reaches toward its single-pointed cap-stone, all separate issues in life are resolved in one great higher truth. Whether our movement is through the spiritual rigor of prayer or the mental rigor of science, the uppermost end of our journey is the love of God. So say some already: after reading this book, many more will agree. Join them.

One doesn't have to believe in any religion or buy into any dogma. Scientifically minded, rational eyes will do, for Katra and Targ have made sure of it. They hold a candle up for everyone, and in its light is revealed a much expanded, more unified world within and without. Every road is a mountain road, and there turns out to be only one mountain.

The peak, as you shall see in this book, is spectacular — scientif-ically sound as well as absolutely miraculous. Katra and Targ provide a wonderful view.

— Marianne Williamson

Acknowledgments

I t gives us great pleasure to thank the many friends, colleagues, and teachers who have encouraged, informed, and inspired us throughout the writing of this book. In particular we want to thank: Our patient friend Dr. Dean Brown for generously sharing his insights and profound scholarship; Dr. William Braud for decades of fundamental research into the nature of distant mental influence of living systems; Judy Skutch Whitson for her vision, trust, and commitment to the publishing and translation of *A Course in Miracles;* Drs. Jerry Jampolsky and Diane Cirincione for teaching a meaning of forgiveness that has promoted worldwide peace and understanding; and Dr. Elisabeth Targ for her dedication and pioneering research on distant healing in the hospital.

Thanks also to Dr. Bob von Gutfeld for decades of thoughtful conversation about the meaning of it all, and a lifetime of friendship; the late Dr. Ross Katra, for his love and valiant search for spirituality, and for providing the inspiration for this book by asking why scientists pray; Ingo Swann, Joe McMoneagle, and Gary Langford for their indefatigable efforts and generous sharing of their remote viewing talent; Rev. Marge Britt for her gifts of vision and inspiration; Father Thomas Keating for his lifetime commitment to teaching how to find peace; Rev. Stan Hampson for his continuing insight and inspiration; Phyllis Butler and Jason Gardner for their thoughtful and painstaking efforts in editing this book; Peggy Leising, and Drs. Jeffrey Mishlove and Arthur Hastings for generously taking the time to read and critique early manuscripts; our agent, Doug Latimer, for helping to make this book a reality; Marc Allen for believing that our ideas were worth sharing and publishing; and most especially to Gangaji, for acquainting us with *sat-chit-ananda* so that we didn't kill each other during the writing of this book.

Introduction

The Search for a Comprehensible Spiritual Life

All day I think about it, then at night I say it.
Where did I come from,
*   and what am I supposed to be doing?*
I have no idea.
My soul is from elsewhere, I'm sure of that,
*   and I intend to end up there.*
*   — Rumi*

The quests for meaning and peace of mind compel us all. These heartfelt desires are the subject of this book. Why do we feel greater peace sitting in a seaside cabin in the midst of a tumultuous thunderstorm than sitting at the dinner table with our loving family in suburban San Francisco? And how was it possible for psychiatrist and writer Viktor Frankl to find meaning and spirit amidst the atrocities and suffering of a Nazi concentration camp? Both of these questions teach us that to experience meaning in our lives, we must focus our attention beyond the consciousness of our separate self.

Clearly, we perceive something greater than ourselves in the power of a raging thunderstorm. Unable to schedule, organize, or control it, we can only surrender to the experience. The storm declares, "Here I am. I'm in control — you just let go!" And *what* we release, if only for a moment, is our usual focus on ourselves: our body, our thoughts, emotions, desires, memories, imagination — even our fears. We are given a rare opportunity to stop the continual chatter of our minds. Rather than anguishing about future or past events over which we have no control, we become still and simply experience the present.

During his three years in Auschwitz and other concentration camps, Frankl discovered that the prisoners who survived transcended their own suffering, shared their meager food, and focused their attention on relieving the misery of prisoners around them. Frankl even found kindness among the German guards. Today, as we approach the end of this frantic and materialistic century, Frankl's message is to open our hearts or perish. He wrote that even under the torturous conditions of the death camps people had the spiritual freedom to choose the attitudes they wished to embody. "It is this spiritual freedom — which cannot be taken away — that makes life meaningful and purposeful," he wrote. [1]

We have written this book to describe a comprehensible spirituality, one in which experience takes primacy over religious belief. We are in part responding to a recent book, *The Demon-Haunted World*, written by one of the most notable scientists of the twentieth century, Carl Sagan. In that book, Sagan stirred together flying saucers, crop circles, alien abductions, *and* God, declaring that he finds them all incomprehensible.

We base our response to Sagan on a description of the *experience* of God, rather than a doctrine of belief. As scientists we are convinced that a person need not *believe* or take on faith anything about the existence of universal spirit, because the *experience* of God is a testable hypothesis. Philosophical proof, however, is not at all the purpose of this book. Instead, we offer a plausible argument to anyone seeking a spiritual life who, at the same time, desires to remain a critical and discerning participant in the twenty-first century. We can include God in our lives without giving up our minds, if we can transcend our usual analytical thoughts and learn to become *mindful*.

In his 1939 essay "Science and Religion," Albert Einstein wrote that we each have the potential for a greater awareness of truth than analysis alone can provide: "Objective knowledge provides us with powerful instruments for the achievements of certain ends. But, the ultimate goal itself, and the longing to reach it, must come from another source." [2]

Although we are experts in neither philosophy nor theology, we offer our experiences and observations with the hope that readers may become *knowers* as opposed to *believers,* and find new appreciation for their innate power of attention. We hope readers will discover their powerful potential as spiritual alchemists of the universe.

One of us, Jane, earned her doctorate degree in health education at the University of Oregon, where she taught nutrition and health classes for many years. She has also practiced spiritual healing for over twenty years, following instructions she received in 1974 during a period of prolonged physical pain accompanied by a near-death-like dream. The culmination of an extended trip Jane took through Southeast Asia, her experience happened while she was observing spiritual healers in the Philippines. She presently works as an "immune system coach," helping her clients to "change the host (themselves) so the disease doesn't recognize them." She helps people change what they feed their mind and heart, as well as their body and soul.

The other author, Russell, is an internationally known laser physicist and psychic researcher. He cofounded the government-sponsored ESP research program at Stanford Research Institute (SRI), documenting the existence of human psychic abilities in the 1970s and 1980s. He began his investigations of extrasensory perception as a result of his own ESP experiences while performing as a stage magician during college. Often when he was pretending to read the mind of someone in the audience, he would receive a clear mental picture of the person's distant home environment — a white house with a brick facade, for example, or the details of their bedspread pattern, or the arrangement of living room furniture. Many well-known professional magicians — some who hate having to deal with ESP — have reported similar occurrences.

In addition to our shared scientific background, we have been students of the Perennial Philosophy and *A Course in Miracles* for many years, and have been blessed with the opportunity to study with inspiring spiritual teachers of Christian, Theosophical, and Buddhist paths, as well as in the self-inquiry tradition of the Indian sage Ramana Maharshi.

We have detailed our remote viewing and spiritual healing experiences in our book *Miracles of Mind*. We hope here to expand on these topics to show how modern scientific evidence of parapsychological phenomena fits with millennia of mystical wisdom teachings. We seek to explore the rich intersection of mysticism and parapsychological science, and to show how they both represent an experience of God that is available to us all.

Wisdom teachers throughout history have shown that the experience of God is possible without belonging to a church or following a religion, as long as one's basic motive is to discover truth. Dr. Herbert Benson recently proposed that we — our bodies and our brains — are "hardwired for God." By this he means that throughout the past twenty-five hundred years — from Buddha, Jesus, and the Baal Shem Tov (the founder of Hassidic Judaism), to such poets as Blake, Emerson, and Rumi, to the Maharishi's contemporary transcendental meditators — mystics have shared a common experience that is actually available to us all.

Contemporary writers have stressed the commonality of this experience. In her encyclopedic *A History of God*, Karen Armstrong calls us all *Homo Religiosus*. "Men and women started to worship gods as soon as they became recognizably human," she writes. [3] In his most recent book, *The Marriage of Sense and Soul*, Ken Wilber identifies the Great Chain of Being as a teaching common to almost every religious belief system. "According to this nearly universal view," he writes, "reality is a rich tapestry of interwoven levels, reaching *from matter [physics] to body [biology] to mind [psychology] to soul [theology] to spirit [mysticism].* Each senior level 'envelops' or 'enfolds' its junior dimensions." [4]

Whenever we sit peacefully on a rock and quiet our mind, we have an opportunity to experience an oceanic connection with something outside our separate self. To many, that connection is experienced as an overpowering feeling of love, and it may well constitute part of our evolutionary process as a species.

A feeling of universal love, without any particular object, is often associated with the realization that we reside within an extended community of spirit enveloping all living beings. Such feelings of unbounded, interconnected consciousness have been described by many as an experience of God. The gift of a quiet mind allows us to understand what it means to be *in* love, like being *in* syrup, as contrasted with being in love with another person. It is possible to reside in love as a way of life. This experience is the source of the often-heard expression that "God is love," which in an ordinary context is easily dismissed as a simple cliché, or worse, as incomprehensible.

These oceanic, loving, peaceful experiences are examples of the compelling feeling of "oneness" that mystics have been urging us to explore for millennia. Jesus called this state of awareness "the peace that passes all understanding," and a "kingdom which is not of this world." Hindus call it "bliss," or *ananda.* And the Buddha called it a state of "nirvana" or "no-mind," meaning the absence of thoughts disrupting an awareness of indivisible unity.

This state is available to us *now,* while we reside in the world, whether or not we know or follow any religious teachings. This open-hearted experience is beautifully described by Joan Borysenko in her recent book *The Ways of the Mystic:* "When the heart is open, we overcome the illusion that we are separate from one another, and the

Mystery of Divine love wraps us in a cloak of security." [5] She delin-
eates seven different paths to God that people take to express their
spirituality. The paths include the ways of earth and nature, service,
sexuality/creativity, religious observance, contemplation, love and
devotion, and, finally, faith.

The path to God we describe in our book comes through being
still, going nowhere, and doing nothing. It is the way of direct experience, without trying any particular method or believing any special
scripture.

This book did not spring from the authors' beliefs in spiritual or
theological matters. While we are accustomed to reaching conclusions conceptually and intellectually, based on our training in science
and research, the motivation for writing this book is rooted in our
experience and our heart-to-heart connections with our teachers,
rather than in analysis.

Jane, in particular, seeks in this book to explain to readers *before*
they become ill how such a seemingly unscientific and illogical thing
as spiritual healing could possibly be effective, and why she traded
her respectable career in university teaching and research for a life of
meditation, prayer, and spiritual healing. She especially wants to
answer all of her former friends, colleagues, and embarrassed family
members who wonder, "Why is such an intelligent, though obviously not enlightened, person as you doing such a strange thing as *that?*"

Talking about God in the Twenty-First Century

Early in the twentieth century, two of the world's greatest logi-
cians, Ludwig Wittgenstein and Alfred Ayer, wrote respectively
Tractatus Logico-Philosophicus and *Language, Truth and Logic.* These
two enormously influential works attempted to describe the physics
and metaphysics of what can be known about reality. These Logical
Positivists proclaimed that nothing meaningful could be said about
God, because no experiment could be designed to either prove or dis-

prove, verify or falsify, whatever one might say. But by the end of their lives both Wittgenstein and Ayer were willing to seriously examine the idea that the experience of mystics might actually be considered data — something observable in an experiment. In fact, in Wittgenstein's last book, *On Certainty,* he gave primacy to experience over theory.

Philosopher Ken Wilber makes this point with great force in his book *Quantum Questions.* He asserts convincingly that although physics will never explain spirituality, the spiritual realms may be explored by the scientific method. "The preposterous claim that all religious experience is private and noncommunicable is stopped dead by, to give only one example, the transmission of the Buddha's enlightenment all the way down to present-day Buddhist masters" (allowing it to be experienced and discussed today). [6]

For thousands of years wisdom teachers such as the Buddha have presented a worldview to all who will listen. They have described a practice that is available for all to observe and experience. They then invite us to compare our experience, and see if it corresponds to with their teaching. Ultimately, this seems to us like an acceptably scientific, empirical approach to spirituality.

Wilber describes three different, but equally valid, avenues of scientific empiricism: *the eye of the flesh,* which informs us about the world of our senses; *the eye of the mind,* which allows us access to mathematics, ideas, and logic; and *the eye of contemplation,* which is our window to the world of spiritual experience. None of these approaches suggest that we must embrace any body of dogma, or that we need to integrate Santa Claus into a scientific view of the modern world. They do, however, invite us to look beyond our thinking mind to discover who we are.

Indian philosophies teach that the mind is consciousness in motion, and that each person's consciousness is the conditioned aspect of God, which is characterized by Infinite Awareness, or what they call "Self." Our bodies are instruments of cognition and action; we are both the tools and the expression of God's creative energy. "All that lives works for protecting, perpetuating, and expanding consciousness," according to Vedanta sage Sri Nisargadatta Maharaj. 7

Thirty years ago national magazines proclaimed on their covers that "God is dead." Today, we would say that God is neither alive nor dead, but rather manifesting as activity in our consciousness, transcending and transforming our ordinary awareness. In his inspiring recent work *God Is a Verb,* Rabbi David Cooper teaches that God is an active personal experience rather than a distant entity in the sky, and that we ourselves are creatures *God-ing* as we express ourselves. Our five familiar senses bring us data of the material world, while filtering out and limiting our exposure to the wider, transcendent world of active awareness available to the quiet mind.

In this book, we do not address the Judeo-Christian God, the "Creator of the Universe" that many have difficulty experiencing. We are happy to leave the question of creation to astronomers and theoreticians who devote their lives to studying first causes. A recent *Newsweek* cover story entitled, "Science Finds God," quoted Carl Sagan as saying that because the laws of physics now explain the birth of the universe, there is "nothing for a Creator to do," and every thinking person is therefore forced to admit "the absence of God." 8 Although we again disagree with Sagan, we are reminded of a Buddhist story regarding this eternal question: A student once asked the Buddha, "Why did God create the universe?" He replied, "That is not your problem. What is *your* problem?"

What we do address in these pages are vital issues of human consciousness — how contemporary scientific research relates to the spiritual life. In Chapter 3 we explore the laboratory data for our expanded self, not as metaphysical theory, but as demonstrated by the existence of *nonlocal mind:* consciousness unimpeded by the limitations of time and distance. Ian Stevenson's extensive investigations of children's previous-life memories, suggesting survival of some aspect of consciousness after the death of the body, are described in Chapter 4.

In Chapter 5 we present recent hospital research data supporting both spiritual healing and the efficacy of prayer. Investigations of these phenomena offer the "sense data" Wittgenstein and Ayer wanted in their discussion of God. The possibility of finally meeting their requirements is the core idea of this book, an approach influenced by the fascinating, technical treatment of these epistemological issues presented in Malcolm Diamond's anthology *The Logic of God.*

In Chapter 6 we explain why a scientist — or any thoughtful person — might want to explore prayer. Chapter 7 describes how we create our life experiences through the way we choose to invest our attention. Here, we invite our readers to consider the idea that the direction of our attention is the most powerful tool we have to transform our lives.

In Chapter 1, we explore the illusion of separation, what the mystics have said about it, and how this experience transcends the analytical approach favored by science. In Chapter 2, we examine the Perennial Philosophy — how we can find common mystical truths in all the wisdom traditions and religions, but that we don't need them to find the experience of God.

Throughout this book we show that no conflict exists between the experience of God and modern science. In fact, the ability to experience God occurs in a state of awareness that transcends the analytical mind's ability to comprehend. In the early 1800s, the distinguished French astronomer Pierre-Simon Laplace taught that all future events could be known if we knew the position and velocity of every particle in the universe. Science has much greater humility today. The Uncertainty Principle, sometimes known as the Principle of Indeterminacy, is a fundamental concept in modern quantum physics, discovered in the 1920s by Werner Heisenberg. It shows that it is *impossible* to know both the exact position and velocity of even a single atom.

In mathematics, the most significant proof, and possibly the most far-reaching idea of this century, is Gödel's Incompleteness Theorem, which shows that *every* axiomatic or mathematical system has at least one proposition whose truth or falsity *cannot be determined.*

Most recently, physicist David Bohm has written extensively about nonlocality in physics, a scientific model supporting the idea that the separation of each person's consciousness is an illusion. Bohm demonstrates that all objects in the universe interact with one another, no matter what the apparent distance between them. 9 His model, which he calls "quantum interconnectedness," portrays reality as a vast, interconnected hologram.

After centuries of academic bombast, we are finally coming to recognize how tentative so-called scientific truth really is. In a scientific world increasingly governed by laws of "indeterminacy," "incompleteness," and "nonlocality," we are beginning to find plenty of room for the experience of God.

Many writers on religious or spiritual issues insult the intelligence of thoughtful people by asking them to believe things they instinctively feel could not possibly be true, or are simply incomprehensible. This often leaves people angry, frustrated, and skeptical, with no inspiration to pursue a spiritual life.

People everywhere are searching for ways to bring meaning into their stressful lives. Our days are filled with an increasing number of activities, and a decreasing amount of time in which to do them. We look for happiness through the desperate acquisition of *things*. We want things now, and we want them to last forever. Despite owning more possessions than any people in history, despite our advanced learning, sophisticated communication, and technological apparatus, our lives are overshadowed by feelings of isolation, despair, and powerlessness. And we feel this during the greatest period of prosperity and good health in history. We feel unable to change the course of our individual lives, our communities, or our environment, where life often seems hopelessly threatened.

It is obvious that suffering is universal — certainly not limited to any particular life circumstance. And yet, the message of spiritual teachers throughout history has been that pain, crises, and despair are potentially powerful initiators in the essential discovery of who we are. This discovery is the experience of a state of awareness that cannot be reached — only *recognized* as our true nature, which is infinite and unbounded consciousness. According to spiritual teacher Gangaji:

> We have tried everything to get rid of suffering. We have gone everywhere to get rid of suffering. We have bought everything to get rid of it. We have ingested everything to get rid of it.
>
> Finally, when one has tried enough, there arises the possibility of spiritual maturity with the willingness to stop the futile attempt *to get rid of,* and, instead, to actually experience suffering. In that momentous instant, there is the realization of that which is beyond suffering, of that which is untouched by suffering. There is the realization of who one truly is. [10]

The Perennial Philosophy first described by Aldous Huxley is the thread of universal truth that permeates all the world's spiritual traditions. It teaches us that alongside the actions we take to improve our world, we also have the opportunity to experience either unity and peace or isolation and fear. While we can't always control the events around us, we do have power over *how* we experience those events. At any moment, we can individually and collectively affect the course of our lives by choosing to direct our attention to the aspect of ourselves that is aware, and to awareness itself. The choice of where we put our attention is ultimately our most powerful freedom. Our choice of attitude and focus affect not only our own perceptions and experiences but also the experiences and behaviors of others.

Mahatma Gandhi taught that "The only devils in the world are those running around in our own hearts. That is where the battles should be fought." Heaven and Hell are available for the asking, but no experience can take place in our lives except in *our* consciousness, with *our* agreement.

A master told his student: "You don't have to look for God. God is here now. If you were ever here, you would see him." Of course, God is neither a "him" nor someone to be seen. But the lesson of awareness is powerful. We seek in this book to make the experience of God available. While religious dogma has often made God unattainable, and incomprehensible, our goal is to provide a framework in which even those who view the world analytically can participate in a meaningful and inspiring spiritual life.

CHAPTER

1

Make Me One with Everything

The Illusion behind Our Feelings of Separation

At the end of our wanderings there is only
the soul's yearning to return to God.
— Ram Dass

Why bother with God? People often say they turn to God and religion to find peace and make sense of the world. Of course, the question of whether God exists rarely enters into that decision. But if God does exist, why wouldn't a smart guy like Carl Sagan know about it? We probably could say that for Sagan, science was his religion — his chosen path to finding answers to life's important questions. Unfortunately, science can only resolve a certain class of questions: those that deal with the physical world. Science cannot help us answer questions of the heart, such as finding a sweetheart, peace of mind, or the meaning of life. And you can't use science itself to prove that science is the right path to find the answer.

As we suggested in our introduction, many of us have learned from the Logical Positivists like Ayer and Wittgenstein that if something isn't either verifiable or falsifiable by the scientific method, we should consider it unworthy of our attention, or even nonsense. But science *itself* is based on the unverifiable premise that it is the most

appropriate method for discovering truth. Sagan failed to look outside his self-prescribed domain for answers to the God problem. Like
a man repeatedly searching for his lost keys under the light of a familiar lamppost, Sagan also neglected to examine the areas of science
that would have illuminated the answers.

Of course, we are all indebted to this great scientist for his
accomplishments and for introducing an entire generation to the
adventures of the universe. His gifts as an educator and scientist
point precisely to why both his dismissals and his admissions about
spirituality are so important. In his last book before he died, *The
Demon-Haunted World,* Sagan acknowledged the possibilities for further study of our interconnected nature. He wrote: "There are three
claims in the ESP field which, in my opinion, deserve serious study:
(1) that by thought alone humans can (barely) affect random number
generators in computers; (2) that people under mild sensory deprivation can receive thoughts or images "projected" at them; and (3) that
young children sometimes report the details of a previous life, which
upon checking turn out to be accurate and which they could not
have known about in any other way than reincarnation." [1]

We examine these very areas in Chapter 3 as key ingredients of a
comprehensible spirituality, taking Sagan's own words as inspiration:
"Science is not only compatible with spirituality, it is a profound
source of spirituality." [2] Unfortunately, Sagan's spirituality includes
neither the existence nor the experience of God.

We believe that precisely these areas of ESP research point to an
activity and power in the universe beyond our separate selves. The
first element he mentions is that thoughts have effects — effects that
have been strongly demonstrated in double-blind, hospital-based
studies of the efficacy of prayer. These recently published experiments of Drs. Elisabeth Targ and Randolph Byrd in "distant healing"
were successful with both AIDS and cardiac patients. Prayer appears to

manifest the power in the universe that many people associate with the existence of God.

The second part of ESP or psi research that Sagan found interesting was the fact that people can receive thoughts and impressions from outside themselves. This area of study has been the subject of two decades of remote viewing research at Stanford Research Institute, in which hundreds of ordinary people learned to experience and describe distant events and locations that were blocked from ordinary perception. From our personal experience with these scientifically demonstrated mind-to-mind connections, we are confident that making contact with at least one element of our spiritual community is not difficult. This element is the unbounded consciousness we all share, that interconnects us throughout space and time. Following the model of physicist David Bohm, we refer to this extended awareness that transcends time and space as our *nonlocal mind.* As we mentioned earlier, Bohm calls it quantum interconnectedness. This interconnectedness is what makes it possible for us to experience being part of a spiritual community.

The idea of connecting with our community is by no means just a religious prescription. In the 1980s, Stanford University, with their large, research-oriented hospital, noticed that the engineers at Lockheed Missiles & Space Corporation were having more than their share of heart attacks. Stanford psychologists interviewed the survivors to investigate their coping styles and strategies. They asked these men, "How many close friends do you have, with whom you can discuss your most important issues?" The most frequent answer to this question, was "zero." Learning this astonishing fact from the researcher who conducted the study was one of our motivations for writing this book about connections.

Finally, Sagan's third point about ESP: Psychiatrist Ian Stevenson has collected thousands of reports from children all over the world who have described their memories of previous lives to their parents. These children are able to guide their parents to their earlier-life homes and identify previous friends, spouses, and children, often with outbursts of profound and appropriate emotions.

We devote a later chapter to each of these potentially important elements of a spiritual life. Each demonstrates that our separation is an illusion, and that there is more to us than our physical bodies.

Sagan never wanted to *believe* in God — he wanted to *know*. But in order to discover God, Sagan would have had to stop thinking and talking long enough to hear what other great minds before him had to say. He would have had to stop his own racing thoughts, brilliant as they were, to allow new knowledge to enter his consciousness. Not all truth is realized through the intellect, no matter how great that intellect is. And science, as well as organized religion, has failed to give people the tools they need to experience God.

We are in complete agreement with Sagan on one position: "The very act of understanding is a celebration of joining, merging . . . with the magnificence of the Cosmos. And the cumulative worldwide buildup of knowledge over time converts science into something only a little short of a transnational, transgenerational meta-mind."[3]

We would say we are all *imbedded in* and share a magnificent meta-mind known as consciousness. Throughout more than three thousand years, in all parts of the world, mystics have described their experience of merging with this "meta-mind" as a joining with God. It has been repeatedly described as the experience of universal love — a description far more enduring and stable than much of our so-called scientific truth.

The scientific picture of the world changes constantly. Ptolemy, a scientist of ancient Greece, was able to predict the motions of the planets quite correctly, even though he mistakenly placed the earth at the center of the solar system. Newton obviously contributed tremendous understanding to physics, but he thought that space was an absolute frame of reference — like some giant clock. Einstein's theory of relativity proved this concept incorrect, and Heisenberg proved that *all* measurements are uncertain, especially at the quantum level. Every day some new surprising or contradictory fact about the world comes to light. Even the age of the universe has been reassessed after globular clusters of stars were recently discovered to be older than the firmly established date of the Big Bang.

But when the mystics quiet their minds, their descriptions give us the impression that they have visited similar places and have had similar experiences. The eminent empiricist philosopher C.S. Pierce wrote an entire paper arguing that this unanimity of mystical experience throughout history was "A Neglected Argument for the Reality of God."

Because of its great successes, science has served much of the Western world as a religion. It has lit our houses and kept us warm. It has provided us with travel, communication, and entertainment. It has doubled our life span in the last century. And it has given us an increasingly comprehensible picture of the physical universe. Ultimately, science has given us enormous quantity for our minds, but not necessarily quality for our hearts.

Beyond Science: Experience

So, what's new in our worldview? The amazing truth is that we reside in a world that is like an ocean filled with love. We know this is an incomprehensible and unscientific-sounding proposition. Although most of us sense it occasionally, very few of us actually realize its profound possibilities. We catch only glimpses of it now and then. We may intuitively feel that as long as we remain entrenched in our isolated selves, we are missing something important in our lives. But when we finally experience this important missing piece of the puzzle, we understand why we're here — and how we are meant to be living.

The feelings of peace, love, and connection that are available to the quiet mind have been described by mystics and poets from Buddha and Rumi, to Emerson and Whitman. They tell us that we can experience the world as a brighter, more loving place, if we can stop running on automatic. They say the only way to take control of your mind is to learn to shift for yourself.

The Experience of Suffering Is Optional

A core tenet of Buddhism teaches that even though our lives are filled with painful events, our suffering is optional and unnecessary. We all experience negative emotions, confused thinking, and real pain, but we don't have to experience these as suffering. We have the opportunity to notice them — and to let them go. One of us had an opportunity to personally discover that if you can focus your attention exquisitely in the present, even fear of death will disappear.

Early in 1997, Russell found himself at Columbia Presbyterian Hospital in New York City suffering from serious and mysterious bleeding. He describes his experience: I was being cared for by three doctors in whom I had great confidence. But as I looked up at these wise men standing at the foot of my bed, it was clear they didn't know what to do. With tears in my ears, I faced the real possibility that I might soon die. As night fell, I remembered the teaching that surrender is not the same as giving up. I quit trying to run my own case and surrendered to the universe to follow its course. I pursued the well-known mantra "Let go, let God" and listened, with my full attention, to the Haydn string quartets a good friend had brought me.

As I became more and more involved with the music, my fear diminished. As I followed the music measure by measure, the fear disappeared entirely! The scientist part of me was astonished. I discovered I could increase and decrease my experience of fear by opening and closing the temporal width of my window of attention.

Realizing that the present moment is free of fear, I went to sleep and awoke the next day on the road to recovery.

The important lesson for me was that both fear and depression reside in the future, based on impressions from the past. The opportunity to change our mind and find peace, meaning, and love in the midst of strife has been taught for thousands of years. The reason it has fallen into neglect in this scientific age is that the path resides in *experience* rather than analysis. As a good scientist, Sagan denies the value of experience, saying, "Miracles are attested, but what if they're instead some mix of charlatanry, unfamiliar states of consciousness, misapprehensions of natural phenomena, and mental illness?" 4

Indeed, as recently as 1996, the official psychiatric diagnostic inventory, DSM-IV, considered the idea that "sometimes people can read my thoughts" to be evidence of mental illness, all by itself. Although this idea is still suspect, other indications are necessary today in order to commit someone to the hospital. We, on the other hand, believe that mind-to-mind connections, rapport, empathy, and feelings of oneness are all part of a transcendent path that leads to peace and meaning.

Karen Armstrong explains in *A History of God* that experiencing God allows us to "feel connected to all and everything." 5 Now, you may feel no desire whatsoever to be any more connected to certain family members, coworkers, or neighbors than you already are. But what if there were something that could ease the sadness that comes from feeling so separate and isolated? What if there were a way of being alone in the stillness, without being in fear? Would you not embrace this feeling of unity — of wholeness?

Once a person has accumulated accomplishments and rooms full of stuff, and has moved to a bigger place to accommodate it all, what next? Remodel? Travel? Get a more powerful car and a larger TV? In California, the answer is usually to remodel, which is an opportunity to focus one's attention on an overwhelming variety of external hardware, instead of looking at the mess inside.

Opportunities for Distraction Are Limitless

Psychologist Charles Tart recently said, "The opportunities to distract ourselves are greater than ever — so great, in fact, that you never *have to* have a quiet moment alone with your own mind again."[6] But we pay a price for such distractions from our true selves.

After all the doing and having, what about exploring alternative ways of *being?* What exotic regions of our own consciousness lie dormant and undiscovered? Seeking an experience of God means cultivating deeper and grander states of awareness than most of us normally experience as we hurry along automatically reacting to our lives.

Many people who long ago turned their backs on organized religion also excluded the possibility that behind all the unbelievable dogma and rituals was a valuable *experience* of God that was worth investigating. Each religious path, conditioned by time and tradition, teaches its own approach to the same ineffable experience. The Indian spiritual teacher Sri Maharaj Nisargadatta said, "Religion is the tracks where something alive once passed — follow the tracks to their source."[7] He told his students to turn their minds to measure the depth of the silence, the stillness which exists prior to thought, beneath their active suffering.

Western spiritual seekers of truth can choose to consciously cultivate what Eastern spiritual traditions describe as "mindfulness" by developing what psychologist and meditation teacher Jon Kabat-Zinn calls "an intimacy with stillness." In his book *The Essential Mystics,* Andrew Harvey asserts that true spirituality is not about passive escape from earthly living, but rather about active arrival *here,* "in full presence." He describes the experience of oceanic love available to the quiet mind:

It always transcends anything that can be said of it, and remains always unstained by any of our human attempts to limit or exploit it. Every mystic of every time and tradition has awakened in wonder and rapture to the signs of this eternal Presence and known its mystery as one of relation and love. [8]

Arrival at Mystical Awareness

So how does one arrive? How do we experience our spiritual community? We do it by becoming aware of unity consciousness: the interconnectedness of our individual selves. All wisdom traditions teach that the separation of our consciousness from one another is a misperception or illusion. The world's spiritual teachings all seek the same objective. They tell us:

"The kingdom of God is within you." — Christianity
"Look within, thou art the Buddha." — Buddhism
"God dwells within you as you." — Yoga
"Atman (individual consciousness) is Brahman (universal consciousness)." — Hinduism
"He who knows himself, knows his Lord." — Islam [9]

I, Russell, have often heard that God is love, which I thought was just something Christians say to annoy the nonbelievers. But, it is possible to unpack this little bundle of wisdom. I now understand it as the *experience* of overpowering love that results from being in contact with a spiritual essence greater than myself. This blissful feeling transcends my knowledge of the limits of space and time. It is an experience out of time — without future projects or past regrets.

Most important is that the oceanic, overwhelming love the mystics describe is love *without an object.* The life force that animates one's being *is* this love. For me it was a life-changing gift that created a feeling of overpowering gratitude and spontaneous appreciation for all life, even people I thought I disliked. This love even includes the self-love, the love at one's core, that is ordinarily hard for anyone to realize. With this awareness, one's personal self expands beyond its personality, memories, and life story to see itself connected to all living beings.

I realized that this love is the gravity that attracts us all, and holds us together in a community of interconnectedness. Just as I can't be a musician by thinking about music, I can't know God or love by simply exercising my intellect. Tibetan Buddhist teacher Sogyal Rinpoche tells us: "The absolute truth cannot be realized within the domain of the ordinary mind. And the path beyond the ordinary mind, all the great wisdom traditions have told us, is through the heart. This path of the heart is devotion." [10]

Spiritual teachers say that to establish and maintain any relationship, affectionate awareness — the willingness to connect — must be expressed. The same is true for maintaining a relationship with infinite consciousness, known as God.

Charles Tart has written extensively on what he calls "state specific knowledge" — that certain kinds of knowledge are only available in corresponding states of awareness. The problem is, I discovered I have to be willing to give up my personal suffering to experience this state-specific dimension of the spiritual. As a scientist I was as afraid of surrendering my analytical mind to the state of selfless love as I was of experiencing death. Overwhelming love sounded to me like uncontrolled intimacy, and losing control.

Spiritual teachers tell us that all of our fears ultimately come down to our fear of death. Because of our materialistic worldview, we are intent on preserving our bodies and everything that goes with them. We associate preserving our wealth with preserving our lives. We fear oneness will interfere with the survival of our separate identity. Wisdom teachers say that this illusion of separateness is precisely the problem.

The core of the Buddhist teaching on this subject, according to life-long meditator and teacher Treya Killam Wilber, is "to ditch the small self." [11]

Self-Knowledge

To study Buddhism is to study the self.
To study the self is to forget the self.
— Dōgen, *The Way of Everyday Life*

Ditching the small self and "loving one's neighbor" are the *result* of self-knowledge, not the cause. And this self-knowledge comes from experience, not books, authority figures, or religious dogma. When we directly experience who we are, from the spiritual perspective of consciousness, we realize that the perception of ourselves as a separate entity has no real independent existence, because our consciousness has no boundaries.

"The true value of a human being is determined primarily by the measure and the sense in which he has attained liberation from the self," Einstein wrote in 1934. "A human being is a part of the whole, called by us 'Universe' — a part limited in time and space. He experiences himself, his thoughts and feelings as something separated from the rest — a kind of optical delusion of consciousness." [12]

The seventeenth-century Dutch philosopher Baruch Spinoza taught the pantheist view that God is omnipresent and unlimited — that is, God is present in us and in *all things*. Spinoza sought to liberate people from fear by teaching that even those things that people and religions perceived as evil were all part of God's perfection. Although Spinoza was excommunicated from his synagogue for his radical views, he was spared death by the Inquisition because he was Jewish. Einstein, three centuries later, when asked if he believed in God, said that he believed in the God of Spinoza: "the organizing principle of the universe." We can clearly see Einstein's mystical perspective in his writing:

> The most beautiful experience we can have is the mysterious. It is the fundamental emotion which stands at the cradle of true art and science. Whoever does not know it and can no longer wonder, no longer marvel, is as good as dead, and his eyes are dimmed. [13]

What Path Leads to Peace?

In twenty-first century terms, we need only to boot-up our minds to participate in the psychic internet to which we are *already* connected, thus overcoming the delusion of separation. Each of the major religions has the same goal: to provide us with a way to know and experience God. The only difference lies in the instructions for accomplishing this knowing.

Millions of people throughout the world have found God through the Vedas, the Bhagavad Gita, the Torah, the New Testament, and the Koran. The formal doctrine taught by each religion can be viewed, without disrespect, as a kind of "sacramental software." The original intent of each religion was to offer us a sacrament or ritual to allow us to experience and talk with God. Think of it: For countless centuries we have been fighting holy wars over software!

When Ken Wilber writes of the various spiritual paths he says, "They are not beliefs, not theories, not ideas, not theologies, and not doctrines. Rather they are vehicles; they are experiential practices. They are experiments to perform. . . . "[14]

Here in Silicon Valley, by the shores of beautiful San Francisco Bay, we live in a world of technology and restaurants. Many residents of this wildly prosperous region focus desperately on money, bodies, and stuff. The tragedy of our prosperity is that while diverse opportunities for making money are everywhere, making, giving, and receiving *love* often receive a lower priority — the proliferation of personal ads not withstanding. In the economic downturn of the 1980s, many high-flying men and women lost their condos and were forced to sleep in their BMWs.

In the last large project I, Russell, worked on as an aerospace scientist, my group was given a billion dollars to install a very powerful laser on a Boeing 747 aircraft to shoot down scud missiles. This project employed locally about one hundred scientists and engineers who worked together in profound disharmony and disrespect. On one occasion a colleague told me, "There was so much fear at that meeting, you could smell it when you walked into the room." My particular motivation for writing this book is to help my brothers and sisters in aerospace to find a way to choose again — to choose gratitude for our fine lives instead of fear.

People are afraid of missing deadlines, exceeding budgets, failing to meet impossible technical requirements, reaching career dead-ends, or losing their jobs. All of these concerns derive from a feeling of scarcity. In Silicon Valley, people are much more frightened of poverty than of death or illness. At one point in my life, I was in such a crisis of meaninglessness and desperation, I was purposely riding my motorcycle without a helmet, with the idea that if I were killed it wouldn't be my fault. I eventually realized that living in a wheelchair with a fractured skull would not greatly improve my life prospects.

We in the aerospace slave pits are worried about a myriad of problems: paying our mortgages, scraping together college tuition, finding a mate, and whether Jerry Rice of the San Francisco 49ers will be able to play the next game. The drawing below from the *Utne Reader* is a shockingly realistic portrayal of many males' consciousness: equal thirds for sex, career, and sports. While these charts are funny, they are also depressingly true depictions of the way many of us live: a path to desperation. As an active member of society, it's very hard to know where to focus my attention to find peace. I am sad to discover that I can't find it in my morning *New York Times.*

I have learned from decades of pain amidst plenty that nothing will ever *make* me happy. Happiness cannot be found or achieved. It is a *process,* and a self-determined state of mind. The thrilling, happy event I've longed for, when it finally occurs, is over in an instant. Then I return to my previous state of mind — whatever it was. Statements and thoughts that begin, "I will finally be happy, when . . ." are simply false. For instance, amazingly, more lives are ruined than saved by winning the lottery. Divorce and bankruptcy are far more common a result than bliss or financial freedom. This may explain, as professor of religion Robert Thurman has suggested, the growing number of celebrity Buddhists, who have realized that their ultimate goals of fame and wealth did not bring happiness.

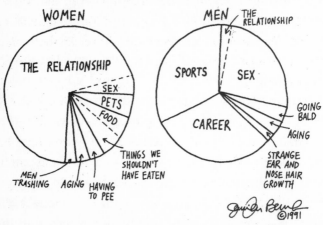

In his groundbreaking book *Flow,* psychologist Mihaly Csikszentmihalyi interviewed thousands of individuals about their inner-life experience. From these data, he describes people's sources of happiness:

> What I "discovered" was that happiness is not something that happens. It is not the result of good fortune, or random chance. It is not something that money can buy or power command. It does not depend on outside events, but rather on how we interpret them. Happiness, in fact, is a condition that must be prepared for, cultivated and defended privately by each person. *People who learn to control inner experience, will be able to determine the quality of their lives, which is as close as any of us come to being happy.* [Emphasis added.] [15]

Philosopher and teacher Andrew Cohen also writes about the search for peace of mind. "Unless the individual is abiding at least 51 percent in that state of not knowing [surrendering] the mind," he writes, *it will be impossible to affect any degree of perfection,* which is the true expression of the ultimate source of being. . . ."[16] In other words, science and analysis are not always the answer.

Many schools of psychoanalysis teach that it is *useless* for the astute therapist to describe a patient's problem to him or her. The patient must experience it. This is very hard for the rational mind to understand. We have to experience the answer at the nonanalytic, visionary, or somatic level of awareness, because that's where the problem resides.

One main problem with many churches and synagogues today is that everyone is comfortable talking *about* God but the silence becomes unbearable when we are asked to *experience* God. The experience of God *is* ineffable and silent. With the increasing desire for a spiritual life throughout America, the awareness is dawning that it requires both facing our discomfort with stillness and being willing to change.

Many people, even scientists, are recognizing that if we perpetually focus our lives on externals, on acquiring things in the future, such as money, possessions, sex, or even death, the result will inevitably be some assortment of desperation, anger, resentment, and fear. Following Andrew Cohen's lead, I have prepared a cartography that maps the territory from desperation to bliss. I am confident about the end points of the chart that we show on the next page. Spending 100 percent of your time thinking about money, bodies, and stuff will definitely lead to desperation. And spending 100 percent of your time experiencing love and connectedness, will likely lead to blissfully floating off the material plane, perhaps because you have forgotten to eat.

I am not foolishly knocking sexuality — quite the contrary. Of course, it nourishes the body, mind, and spirit. We *are* concerned that the materialistic and possessive focus so prevalent in the media, in the locker room, and in ordinary conversation frequently leads to trivialization, pain, and grief.

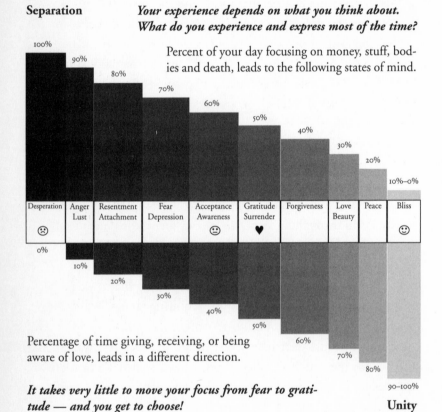

Separation

Your experience depends on what you think about. What do you experience and express most of the time?

Percent of your day focusing on money, stuff, bodies and death, leads to the following states of mind.

Desperation ☹	Anger Lust	Resentment Attachment	Fear Depression	Acceptance Awareness ☺	Gratitude Surrender ♥	Forgiveness	Love Beauty	Peace	Bliss ☺

Percentage of time giving, receiving, or being aware of love, leads in a different direction.

It takes very little to move your focus from fear to gratitude — and you get to choose!

Unity

In this model, the most important step a person can take is from fear toward gratitude. The gratitude is for grace: the *unearned* gifts from God, or the Universe, that make our lives healthier and more abundant than almost any other place or time in the history of the world. I realized that even if my focus is on gratitude for a few moments of the day, I still can spend the other half of my time worrying, analyzing, and resenting. It's not necessary to give up a discerning mind to achieve peace and meaning in life. It seems like a small step, but it had the power to effect great change in my attention, and therefore, in my experience. The most interesting thing about this step is that I didn't have to *do* anything. I just had to change my mind.

For example, when awakening every morning, I have the choice of what mental program to run. I can start the day thinking about bills to pay and jobs to finish, or I can open my eyes and give thanks that I am here for another day, that I enjoy reasonably good health, and that I live in a peaceful community. I had nothing to do with my good fortune to be born in a relatively peaceful country, for example, so being grateful is probably most appropriate.

Now, whom should I thank? For some, there is no question: you thank God. For me, the anthropomorphic view of God is not an entirely helpful answer. The Buddhist would thank his *karma,* the law of cause and effect, which sounds very much like Einstein's "organizing principle of the universe." Others may thank the universe, or the God of love, described by the mystics of all ages. This latter is the manifestation of God that is most easily experienced. Upon awakening in the morning, I can choose: "Life's a bitch and then I die," or "Thank you God, for another day of infinite possibilities." Another difficult decision!

One way to move from fear to gratitude is to consciously cultivate some ritual to help quiet our mental chatter. Such a path might help us experience the unrestrained friendliness the Buddha said flowed easily from a relaxed mind, and to become aware of our true nature, which is unrestrained consciousness. The Buddha taught a prayer that accomplishes all these things. It's called the *metta* prayer, or prayer of loving kindness. Even a skeptical scientist can be comfortable with this 2,500-year-old prayer, because it doesn't require one to believe anything. This brief prayer might also appeal to scientists because of its remarkable efficiency. It addresses in five short lines many of life's principle concerns: peace, love, gratitude, and community.

> May I be in peace.
> May my heart remain open.
> May I awaken to the light which is my true nature.
> May I be healed.
> May I be a source of healing for all beings.

May I be in peace. We can't *have* peace; our challenge is to learn to be peace.

May my heart remain open. This prayer recognizes that our hearts are already open to give and receive love. To reside in this peaceful state it is essential to know how to move out of the separation we tend to foster to assert our beloved individuality and control.

May I awaken to the light of my true nature. Our true nature is love. The universe is filled with consciousness, which animates and inspires each of us, and which we express with our caring attention.

May I be healed. The first step toward healing is to recognize that forgiveness clears our mind space of old animosities.

May I be a source of healing for all beings. In our nonlocal world, if each of us is a center of loving kindness, we can help to heal all beings, or at least those around us, by moving *ourselves* from resentment to respect.

CHAPTER

2

Experiencing God Directly

Spirituality without Religion

"I don't need great faith. I have great experience."

— Joseph Campbell

W hy do we search for God? It may be that our need to lead meaningful rather than absurd lives is even more powerful than our desire to reduce our suffering or to pursue happiness. When physician Herbert Benson claims "We are hardwired for God," he is saying that from the beginning of human life we have reached out for a connection to something greater than ourselves. [1]

Even the earliest societies sought some power outside themselves to provide understanding and control of the inexplicable around them. They worshipped the power of the sun, fire, rivers, storms, even geographical features — all elements most people today consider unconsciousness and thus uncaring.

Maybe more than needing to explain God, our ancestors felt the need to access the power of transcendence. We know, for example, that these early men and women often sang and danced through the night, sometimes while ingesting powerful mind-altering plants, in order to experience a power beyond themselves and their difficult lives. We know that rhythmic body movements sustained for long periods of time also alter consciousness. In more recent times, Sufi Whirling Dervishes, dancers from all cultures, runners, skiers, gymnasts, and other athletes have all found, through movement, a way to stop their ordinary mental processes and experience the overwhelming feeling of oneness available to all who step outside the ordinary. Even children love the thrill of spinning round and round to lose their sense of space, time, and separateness.

Many perceive that *something* meaningful exists beyond their mundane experience of the world, but they usually encounter it only when they fall in love. One reason overpowering feelings of romantic love are so satisfying is that we finally begin to focus our attention outside ourselves. Maybe the secret motivation many mystics have for spending their lives in silence is to experience this feeling of transcendent love all the time! But, the love of God is an unsentimental love with neither an object nor an agenda; the great surprise is that it's available to anyone who takes the time to find it.

Ramana Maharshi, said to be one of the wisest and most enlightened Indian teachers, spent most of his life silently meditating in a mountain cave. One possible answer to why he would do that comes from philosopher Andrew Cohen, who defines enlightenment as the surrender of the ego-mind to the perfection of the cosmos, and the ability to express that perfection. In Christian terms, it might be achieving a self-aware life, walking with God, in what is called "prayer without ceasing." It is, of course, much easier for Maharshi to experience God while peacefully sitting on a rock in India than it is for an overworked engineer at her computer in Silicon Valley, but you have to start the search somewhere.

Maharshi's teaching of self-inquiry guides the seeker on a relentless quest to find and experience God — the love at his or her core. We are instructed to first ask, "Who am I?" — and then, "Who wants to know?" In discussing Ramana Maharshi's contribution, philosopher Lex Hixon writes, "Ramana may be the Einstein of planetary spirituality transcending previous approaches to religion, as the General Theory of Relativity transcended earlier more parochial theories of physics." [2]

The American mystic given the name Gangaji (little Ganges) by her Indian mentor H.W.L. Poonja is a contemporary teacher in the lineage of Maharshi. Gangaji is a beautiful, charismatic woman from northern California who teaches self-inquiry as a path to experiencing the truth. In one of her meetings — called *satsang*, or association with truth — a man in the audience said to her, "You have changed my life. But I don't know what to do. I'm in love with you!" Gangaji replied, more or less, "Of course you're in love. That's okay. But don't get attached to this body or form. As you know, bodies come and go. But I'm happy for you to join me in love. That is your own true nature."

In our experience, Gangaji is an exemplar of one who lives the truth she teaches, and encourages others to join her. She not only teaches the Perennial Philosophy but also demonstrates and transmits for all who spend time with her the experience of a heart bursting with love — what Jesus called, "The love that passes all understanding." She reminds *(re-minds)* anyone so fortunate as to have a transformative heart-bursting experience in her presence that "this limitless love you are now experiencing is always available. *It is who you are.*"[3]

In Chapter 7 we describe this experience of being overcome with love as an orgasm of the heart. It isn't romantic, but an experience of what Buddhists call *sunyata* (emptiness or the absence of independent existence) and Hindus call *Advaita Vedanta* (the truth of not-two). This description of unity consciousness has not changed since before the time of Buddha, who taught, "When your mind is filled with love, send it in one direction, then a second, a third and a fourth, then above, and then below. Identify with everything, without hatred, resentment, anger, or enmity. The mind of love is very wide. It grows immeasurably and eventually is able to embrace the whole world." [4]

The experiences mystics have described since the beginning of history are the focus of what is today called Transpersonal Psychology — psychology beyond the self. Ken Wilber describes it as the part of our being wherein "Spirit knows itself in the form of Spirit." [5] It is not a return to babyhood, where ignorance is undifferentiated sensation and bliss. Rather, it is expanded awareness: where we have the surprising opportunity to realize that loving your neighbor is indeed the same as loving yourself. Jung argued that Freud was seriously mistaken to consider transpersonal experience as a return to the prepersonal "id" of toddlers, who have yet to separate their personalities from their mothers. We agree with Jung: freedom comes from awareness, not ignorance. We discuss these ideas further in Chapter 6.

Once people experience their true nature as transcendent consciousness, connected to all living beings, they may find many things in their life that need changing, in addition to realizing that they themselves are forever changed. As the Hindu saying describes, "Once the elephant has entered the tent, the tent will never be the same."

The Perennial Philosophy

The philosopher Aldous Huxley attempted to distill from the world's religions, with their "confusion of tongues and myths . . . a Highest Common Factor which is the Perennial Philosophy in what may be called the chemically pure state." Huxley wisely warned that "this final purity can never, of course, be expressed by any verbal statement of philosophy." [6] This brings to mind the old aphorism, "Those who know don't say. Those who say don't know." We — each of us — just do the best we can.

In our quest for a comprehensible spiritual life, we have taken Huxley's Perennial Philosophy as the enduring religious elements that stand the test of time and remain with us. We seek to present these elements in a framework that is in agreement with the modern mind's passionate desire for coherence and consistency. We understand that to be successful in interesting a scientist in prayer, we must present an ontology that doesn't offend his or her rational mind. What a task!

We must first acknowledge that science very successfully describes one aspect of human experience: the material universe. On the other hand, science has little to say about many other things we experience, such as love, and spiritual feelings.

These universal feelings, expressed throughout history, have been the source of Huxley's distillation of the world's religious teachings. Here is our understanding of Huxley's four enduring elements of the world's spiritual truth:

1. The world of both matter and individual consciousness is manifested from spirit. The world is more like a great thought than a great machine.

Physicist Amit Goswami has written widely on this issue, teaching that "consciousness is the ground of all being." He writes, "In Quantum Physics, objects are seen as possibilities. . . . It is consciousness, through the conversion of possibility into actuality, that creates what we see manifested. In other words, consciousness creates the manifest world." 7 He goes on to explain, "The universe is self-aware, but it is self-aware through *us.* "

When Jesus taught, "The kingdom of God is within you," he might have meant that the thoughts and consciousness of the entire nonmaterial universe are available to each person's expanded awareness. This ancient truth, combined with Goswami's modern view that "consciousness manifests the world," suggests that we should not be surprised by new scientific evidence for the efficacy of prayer.

2. "Human beings are capable of not merely knowing about the Divine Ground by inference," Huxley writes. "They can also realize

its existence by direct intuition, superior to discursive reasoning." He continues, "This immediate knowledge unites the knower with what is known." For the prophet Muhammad, a philosopher without the *personal experience* of his own philosophy is "like an ass bearing books." In the Koran, God tells Muhammad, "I am closer to you than your jugular vein."

This idea has great contemporary currency in quantum physics. The distinguished American physicist John Archibald Wheeler observed that we live in a participatory universe, where there is little if any separation between the observer and the observed. In parapsychology research, this would be called "direct knowing," for which there is already voluminous evidence from research in mind-to-mind connections, distant healing, remote viewing, and many other areas we describe in the next chapter.

3. Man possesses a dual nature: both an ego associated with our personality and our mortal, physical body, and an eternal spirit or spark of enduring divinity. It is possible, if a person wishes to, to identify with this spirit, and therefore with what Huxley calls "the Divine Ground," or universal consciousness. After more than one hundred years of investigation, compelling evidence now exists that in addition to this divine spark of spirit, *some* aspect of our conscious and unconscious memories survives bodily death. Not that we would put off any current plans for our "next lifetime," but data from children who remember their previous lives is now quite strong, as we will explore in Chapter 4.

4. Finally, the Perennial Philosophy teaches that our life on earth has only one purpose: to learn to unite with the Divine Ground and the eternal, and to help others do the same. Buddhism refers to the *bodhisattva,* a being who has become one with "all that is," and returns to help all living beings. The bodhisattva doesn't distinguish between who is being helped and who is doing the helping because he or she is in a state where there is no separation. As the revered

Vietnamese Zen Buddhist teacher Thich Nhat Hanh reminds us, when the left hand is injured, the right hand does not stop to point out, "now I am taking care of you." [8]

This extension of one's awareness expresses itself as universal love, or a purpose larger than ourselves. As Viktor Frankl writes in his introduction to *Man's Search for Meaning,* "Success, like happiness, cannot be pursued; it must ensue . . . as the unintended side-effect of one's personal dedication to a course greater than oneself." Finally, Brian Swimme writes in his inspiring book *The Universe Is a Green Dragon,* "That our fullest destiny is to become love in human form. . . . Love is the activity of evoking being, of enhancing life. The supreme insistence of life is that you enter the adventure of creating yourself." [9]

This adventure of "evoking being" by "becoming love" echoes the Perennial Philosophy's message of personal transformation of consciousness. It tells us that we are here to learn to unite with the Divine Ground, but it neglects to tell us how to do it. Historically, there have been, and are, many ways to cohere our lives with the teachings of the Perennial Philosophy. These spiritual technologies for uniting one's consciousness with God are teachings that emphasize the experience of God over religious dogma.

Questioning Authority

Most of us have seen the popular 1970s bumper sticker that read, "QUESTION AUTHORITY." A reading of the earliest Buddhist writings illustrates the preeminence that Buddhism gives to direct experience and the questioning of authority. In addressing a group of villagers at Kalamas, the Buddha says:

> Come, O Kalamas, do not accept anything on mere hearsay. Do not accept anything on mere tradition. Do not accept anything on account of rumors. Do not accept anything just because it accords with your scriptures. Do not accept anything merely accounting

for appearance. Do not accept anything just because it agrees with your preconceived notions. Do not accept anything thinking that this ascetic is respected by us.

When you know for yourselves — these things are moral, these things are blameless, these things are praised by the wise, these things when performed and undertaken, conduce to well-being and happiness, then do you live and act accordingly. [10]

These words of 2,500 years ago retain their great wisdom today. Such thinking is the hallmark of a spirituality that moves beyond belief. Don't believe everything you hear, even if it is said by the Buddha. Instead, investigate for yourself and see what is revealed. There is no approximation in direct experience. This is Buddhism's appeal for the questioning mind.

One starting point for such an inquiry are Buddhism's Four Noble Truths. The description we give here comes from the wise and heartful Buddhist teacher Sylvia Boorstein, who is also an observant Jew. The gentle approach in her book *It's Easier Than You Think* is an example of wonderfully applied Buddhism.

The Four Noble Truths have come down to us from 500 BC India. They describe the human condition and make recommendations for bringing meaning to our lives, and in many ways are parallel to Huxley's statement of the Perennial Philosophy. They are also reflected in many of the great religions' esoteric teachings, including Gnostic Christianity and Kabbalistic Judaism.

The First Noble Truth is indisputable: we experience pain because we are aware of the finite, fragile, temporary nature of our lives. Buddhism is a philosophy of self-control of one's mind. If we cannot take charge of our own churning thoughts, how can we take control of our lives in the physical world? As Sylvia Boorstein says, "Pain is unavoidable, but suffering is optional." [11] Suffering comes from the story we attach to the pain — the blaming and dwelling. *A Course in Miracles* teaches a similarly hopeful idea: *"I give all the meaning it has, to everything I experience."* This is how Victor Frankl was able to find meaning and spirituality in a concentration camp.

Suffering is subjective. Consider the following: One of the worst punishments inflicted on prisoners is solitary confinement. At the same time, some people from northern California pay thousands of dollars a month for a similar experience but call it a "silent meditation retreat." The meditator enjoys the experience partially because it's voluntary but also because he or she knows what to do with the mind to create an opportunity out of the solitude, rather than a punishment.

The Second Noble Truth addresses the suffering caused by craving and attachment. It describes how a life lived at the materialistic end of our map of experience in Chapter 1 leads to desperation. This craving for stuff, money, and accomplishments profoundly interferes with our passionate enjoyment of where we are now, in the present. A core Buddhist precept teaches that making distinctions unavoidably leads to both error and suffering. Imprecision inevitably follows when you judge and divide *this* from *that*. Buddha taught this concept from direct observation, and now quantum theory has formulated it into a fundamental "indeterminacy" principle of the universe. We should always remain discerning and courageous in the face of injustice, but *judgment* gets us into trouble — especially judgment of others.

It all goes back to meaning. We can all remember standing with someone in front of a closet full of clothes as he or she cried, "I don't have a thing to wear." And it was true. None of the clothes were new or appealing. They had been drained of meaning, through familiarity, and therefore *were* nothing.

One final insight into the pain of attachment comes from the Tenth Commandment of the Bible. "Thou shalt not covet" is the only commandment that doesn't pertain to deeds. It just deals with thoughts! It's possible that coveting and greed are the most corrosive of all human tendencies, leading to the most anguish and damage to society. And our daily dose of radio and television advertising is one of the greatest sources of this pain. Without doubt, advertising's goal is to create so much desperate coveting that we seek relief by buying and accumulating objects. That's the bad news.

The Third Noble Truth is the terrific good news. As Sylvia Boorstein says, "peace of mind and a contented heart are not dependent on external circumstances." When we take control of our free-running minds, we have the opportunity to *exchange suffering for gratitude:* I may not have solved my life's problems yet, but I can wake up in the morning and focus my attention on gratitude and my connection to the infinite consciousness of the universe, or I can resume my kvetching.

The inspiring story of one man who was able to do this is told by the French writer Jacques Lusseyran in his breathtaking book *And There Was Light.* [12] Lusseyran demonstrated that what you *decide* to focus your attention on is what you get. After losing his sight in an accident at age eight, he relied on his inner resources and the help of devoted friends to complete high school and gain acceptance into university just as World War II was on the horizon.

During the Nazi occupation of Paris, Lusseyran recognized that *information* was the ingredient essential to aiding the Resistance and maintaining people's morale. With his friends, he formed an underground newspaper right under the eyes of the Gestapo. He alone was chosen to interview each potential member of the growing Resistance band because of his unique gift for intuitively determining who could be trusted. Their underground operation continued for two years before they were betrayed by the one person about whom the blind Lusseyran had expressed doubt.

In the concentration camp Lusseyran occupied himself by finding food for the sickest prisoners. Despite his blindness, starvation, and brutal treatment, he helped build a secret radio receiver and became an inspiration to his fellow prisoners. At the end of the war, he was rescued by the Allies, and lived to become a full professor of history at the University of Hawaii. In his autobiography he declares two truths that his remarkable life revealed: "The first of these is that joy does not come from outside, for whatever happens to us, it is within. The second truth is that light does not come to us from without. Light is in us, even if we have no eyes." Once again, the Third Noble Truth reminds us that anything we see and experience has only the meaning that we give it.

The Fourth Noble Truth lays out paths we can follow to find the centered and balanced mental stance that will allow us to take charge of our minds. We describe some of these paths more fully in the final two chapters of this book. Although it is possible to read about these truths, it is vastly preferable to internalize them through contact with an inspired teacher. These roads to happiness and contentment are described in Buddhist terms as the Eight-Fold Path: Right Aspiration, Right Understanding, Right Action, Right Speech, Right Livelihood, Right Effort, Right Concentration, and Right Mindfulness. They are all interconnected, like everything else, but aspiration is the essential first step.

The peace we all wish to experience is achieved through the practice of mindfulness. The only way we know to alleviate our pain, and our longing for love — to be *in* love — is by stopping our fearful mental chatter and taking control of our mind. Mystical traditions teach that the quiet mind is the most available path for anyone seeking to live in love, or to experience a relationship with God, which we think is the same thing.

Yoga and the Mythic Archer

Organized religions invite us to believe that certain words, objects, rituals, leaders, and codified ethical behaviors compose the recipe for getting God to notice and bestow favors on us. One difference between the Buddhist and Hindu approach is that the Hindu religion has a pantheon of Gods, with Vishnu as Creator, and Krishna in his many shapes and guises as his incarnation on earth. And all are one in Brahman — the impersonal absolute. Many Buddhist sects, on the other hand, recognize no God at all. Much of mystical Hinduism is known as Yoga.

Yoga in Sanskrit means unity or "one with God." In Yoga, we are taught that to experience being one with God we simply have to quiet the mind. All the rest is commentary. This is the lesson of one of the most famous scenes in the Bhagavad Gita.

In the opening chapters of the Bhagavad Gita, the sacred Hindu text written in the first or second century AD, Krishna, the son of God, has a conversation with Arjuna, the mythic and heroic archer, in the field of battle. [13] In this poignant scene, Arjuna tells Krishna that he has uncles and cousins on both sides of the battle field, and that he himself is likely to be injured or killed in the battle. Krishna responds: "Do well, whatever you do. You are a soldier, and dying in support of freedom against tyranny is a noble death. And should you die, don't worry, you know that I will see you next time."

"You don't have to read the Upanishads or the Vedas now," Krishna continues. "If you will sit down, stop talking, and quiet your mind, then you will know that God is here with you." This is the fundamental teaching of each of the mystical spiritual paths: Buddhism, Hinduism, Kabbalistic Judaism, Sufism, Gnostic Christianity, and all their modern counterparts. It could be described as the time-tested "sit down and shut up" path to spirituality.

The concept of being still is part of the mystical spiritual wisdom that teaches that personal transformation of consciousness is part of human destiny. The Eastern idea that the purpose of religion is to evoke this transformation began to take hold in the West in the early twentieth century.

Paramahansa Yogananda, as a young Hindu mystic, played a significant role in bringing Eastern spiritual science to the United

States. In 1920, he addressed an international conference of religious leaders on *The Science of Religion.* He taught that religion is whatever motivates all people's actions; religion is "whatever is universal and most necessary for people." Since all people want to avoid pain and attain happiness, a person's religion necessarily consists of these motivations.

Yogananda directly addressed the problem that scientists such as Carl Sagan have in believing in God and other religious concepts:

> Change of forms and customs constitutes for many a change from one religion to another. Nevertheless, the deepest import of all the doctrines of all the different prophets is essentially the same. Most men do not understand this. . . . There is equal danger in the case of the intellectually great: They try to know the Highest Truth by the exercise of the intellect alone; but the Highest Truth can be known only by realization. . . . It is a pity that the intellect or reason of these men, instead of being a help, is often found to be a bar to their comprehension of the Highest Truth. . . . [14]

According to Yogananda, all great wisdom traditions have taught that identification of our true selves with our bodies is a mistaken illusion. We are most truly spirit having bodies for a time, rather than bodies having life or spirit for a time. If we can understand that our "selves" consist of nonlocal consciousness, then we can understand how quieting our body-bound sensations and brain-bound thoughts can help us experience our spiritual essence.

Where Were the Christians?

For centuries, religious scholars have known of the Eastern mystics. But it wasn't until Yogananda spoke in the United States that most Americans became aware of Eastern concepts of mind and consciousness. Helena Blavatsky had already created a significant spiritual movement in the 1890s in Europe, introducing a blend of mysticism (about the direct experience of God) and Hindu Vedanta through her teaching and writing on Theosophy. But it was through

the appearance of the Dead Sea Scrolls and the *Nag Hammadi* discoveries just after World War II that the world became aware of the
roots of mystical Christianity. These early writings of the Gnostic
Christians revealed great similarities between Hinduism and the religious ideas that appeared during the one hundred years following the
death of Jesus. Elaine Pagels, in her *Gnostic Gospels,* dated the origin
of the Gnostic *(Nag Hammadi)* writings, as approximately 50 to 100
AD, contemporary with the Gospels of the New Testament.

In these Gnostic texts, Jesus says, "If you bring forth what is within you, what you bring forth will save you. If you do not bring forth
what is within you, what you do not bring forth will destroy you." [15]

This injunction demonstrates the similarities between the
Gnostic or Christian mysticism and Buddhist, Hindu, and
Kabbalistic writings. Pagels writes that "to know oneself at the deep-
est level is simultaneously to know God; this is the secret of gnosis."
In Pagels' book, another Gnostic teacher, Monoimus says:

> Abandon the search for God and the creation and other matters of
> a similar sort. Look for him by taking yourself as the starting point.
> Learn who is within you, who makes everything his own and says,
> "My God, my mind, my thought, my soul, my body." Learn the
> sources of sorrow, joy, love, hate. . . . If you carefully investigate
> these matters, you will find him within yourself. [16]

The *Gospel According to Thomas* is a fourth-century manuscript
discovered in 1945 near Nag Hammadi in Upper Egypt. It contains
114 sayings of Jesus, showing him as a source of mystical teachings.
The Gospel of Thomas begins, "These are the secret words which
Jesus the living one spoke." Later, we hear the disciples asking Jesus,
"When will the kingdom come?" Jesus replies, "It will not come by
waiting for it. It will not be a matter of saying 'here it is, or there it
is.' Rather, the kingdom of the father is spread out upon the earth for
all to see, but people do not see it." [17]

This teaching reminds us that the kingdom of heaven is here —
available in our *mind* whenever we experience peace and joy. Of

course hell is available in the same place, when we reside in anger and fear. We often stand at a personal crossroads, where one sign says, "This way to Heaven," and the other says, "This way to a workshop on how to get to Heaven." We then have the opportunity to choose again between Heaven now, or Heaven later.

The Gnostic Christians believed they were each one with God, as well as one with the ascended Jesus, and therefore had no need for bishops, priests, or deacons. They would choose their leader each Sunday by drawing straws. The hierarchy of the Church of Rome was outraged that such an important matter should be left to chance, while the Gnostics said, "We leave it up to God." Clement, the Bishop of Rome (c. 90–100), recognized that these free-thinking people were off on their own path. He argued that there is one God, and therefore one Church, and the church of Rome was it.

Gnosticism had the appeal of direct experience. And although the Gnostics were persecuted by the Church of Rome for a thousand years, they continued to find adherents in small and large groups. Then in the middle eleventh century, the Cathari Gnostics, often called the Albigensians because they lived in the Albige (the Toulouse region of southern France), came to the attention of Rome. This ascetic community of almost fifty thousand people shared all their property, and felt they were individually and collectively in continuous communication with God and each other. Rome considered this an intolerable heresy and asked the Noblemen of northern France, including Richard the Lion-Hearted, to make a detour on their Crusade to the Holy Land to kill all the heretic Cathari. In a now-famous exchange of letters, Richard wanted to know how he should determine whom to kill. Pope Innocent III replied, "Kill them all, and God will know his own." This genocide was an early step in what became the Inquisition, and the end of any kind of organized Gnosticism, which was little known until the recent *Nag Hammadi* discoveries and translations.

Kabbalah and the Chain of Being

Judaism has somehow successfully kept their religion alive despite the Diaspora and centuries of persecution. This was accomplished in part through teaching reverence for the Torah as their divinely revealed history and guide. They emphasize a word-by-word and letter-by-letter study of this holy book by each individual, together with constant questioning of its interpretation and meaning. This is how the young Jesus in the Bible was able to address and keep the attention of the Rabbis as he revealed his unique interpretation of the Torah.

One problem for Judaism has been that analysis of the text has often replaced the direct experience of something beyond one's separate self. This omission accounts for the great attraction that Buddhism has for many Jews, because Buddhism offers both an experiential and a comprehensible spirituality. We learn from Roger Kamenetz's fine book *The Jew and the Lotus* that more than one third of all the Buddhist teachers in America are of Jewish origin. Recently, however, a significant number of Jews are becoming familiar with the spiritual aspects of Judaism through the Jewish Renewal movement, which incorporates a new interest in the study of the unity and balance found in the mystic teachings of the Kabbalah. Jewish theologian Rabbi Lawrence Kushner writes:

> Human beings are joined to one another and to all creation. Everything performing its intended task doing commerce with its neighbors. Drawing nourishment and sustenance from unimagined other individuals. Coming into being, growing to maturity, procreating. Dying. Often without even the faintest awareness of its indispensable and vital function within the greater 'body.' . . . All creation is one person, one being, whose cells are connected to one another within a medium called consciousness. [18]

It is thought that the Kabbalah first appeared as a document sometime near the end of the twelfth century. It teaches that every action here on earth affects the entire divine realm, either helping or hindering peace and tranquillity. Kabbalah literally means receiving — making available the received spiritual wisdom of the ancient Jewish mystical tradition. The ten symbols that compose the Kabbalistic "Tree of Life" not only map a spiritual path but also provide a meditative vehicle for potential transcendence. Unfortunately, there is usually more attention paid to the mapping than to the opportunity for transcending thought.

Daniel Matt, in his *Essential Kabbalah,* writes, "Our awareness is limited by sensory perceptions, our minds cluttered with sensible forms. The goal is to 'untie the knots' that bind the soul, to free the mind from definitions, to move from constriction to boundlessness." [19] From his translation of the Kabbalah:

> God is unified oneness — one without two, inestimable. Genuine divine existence engenders the existence of all things. There is nothing — not even the tiniest thing — that is not fastened to the links of this chain. Everything is catenated in its mystery, caught in its oneness. God is one. God's secret is one, all the worlds below and above are mysteriously one. Divine existence is indivisible. The entire chain is one, down to the last link. Everything is linked to everything else. So divine essence is below, as it is above. There is nothing else. [20]

This is an idea revealed through direct experience to a meditating mystic undergoing a unitive experience, similar to that of the Buddhists who teach that "separation is illusion." This compelling feeling of oneness with the universe, and with God, is what motivates people to meditate. Quieting one's thoughts reveals an awareness that our actions have cosmic consequences, in what we do, what we say, and what we think. So, every morning we can choose again: will we be fearful and separate, or grateful and connected?

Towering fear, the so-called terror of the "Dark Night of the Soul" described by Christian mystic John Yepes (known as St. John of the Cross) often precedes and impels surrender to this feeling of oneness. Unity Church teaches, "Let go and let God." Such surrender is acceptance of living in the mystery. Surrender does not mean "giving up"; it is more an awareness and acceptance of our nonlocal consciousness. It entails releasing total control and acknowledging a greater power in the universe than that found in one's separate body.

Faith is another form of acceptance based on the experience — often through prayer — of God in our lives. A silent mind and a receptive and waiting attitude come first, creating an opportunity for transcending thought and separate self. Then faith follows. Faith could be called understanding how the system works. My faith that I can contact my community of spirit when I quiet my mind is based on practice and experience, not on theology, just as my faith that my car will start when I turn the key is based on experience, not something told to me by my Honda dealer.

Science has always had a problem with "faith" in anything but science. But science itself is ever-changing. The sixteenth century Italian philosopher Giordano Bruno was burned alive at the stake for declaring that the earth was not the center of the universe, and today it appears from recent astronomical observations that there may, in fact, be many universes. For a modern physicist, such data come from observing the physical world, and that data changes constantly. Therefore, theories must change. For the mystic, however, the data is his or her experience — and over the past three thousand years the experience of oneness in a quiet mind has been an enduring truth. So, it appears that over the course of millennia, the data of the mystic turns out to be more stable and reliable than the data of the physicist!

The Magic of Mind

We believe that data from contemporary research of psychic abilities — parapsychology — have a part to play in understanding and achieving a useful synthesis of the various mystical experiences described above. We want to emphasize, however, that psychic abilities are *not* necessarily evidence of a person's spiritual attainment or awareness. The data for our extrasensory perception show that our consciousness or spiritual nature transcends the body. This evidence is consistent with the Perennial Philosophy underlying the esoteric teachings of the world's great religions.

Inherent in this universal spiritual philosophy is the idea that human beings are capable of not merely knowing about the Divine Ground by inference but of realizing its existence by direct experience or intuition. This direct knowing is outside the realm of reasoning and analysis. It is possible because, as contemporary physics tells us, we live in a nonlocal universe. And ESP research data show that our consciousness is nonlocal. In the next few chapters we consider three types of experiences in consciousness that demonstrate conclusively our nonlocal nature, unlimited by bodies or time.

The first type of nonlocal evidence we discuss involves the inflowing perceptual experience of something hidden from ordinary perception. This has historically been associated with divination, crystal gazing, or palm reading. In this book we discuss laboratory experiments investigating much more substantial telepathy, clairvoyance, and remote viewing. These forms of direct knowing are ways in which we make contact with our nonlocal universe, uniting the knower with the known. But psychic abilities do not give evidence for a person's spiritual development, any more than ordinary sensory abilities do.

Along with the inflowing of perception is the outflow of intention or will. We have evidence for the human capability of distant psychic healing, parapsychological influence on electronic random number generators, and the ability to change the physiology and heart rate of a distant person by staring at their video image.

Finally, in addition to the inflow of information and outflow of intention, there is the quietness of surrender — doing nothing. The mystics tell us about the psychic experiences that may emerge after quieting the ongoing chatter of our mind. These psychic experiences are available to us as we learn to be still. They demonstrate our mind-to-mind connections throughout space and time but not enlightenment.

Deepak Chopra refers to this ground of awareness in which we are all connected as a dimension of pure potentiality. In his book *The Seven Spiritual Laws of Success,* which draws upon ancient Vedantic wisdom, he writes, "The source of all creation is pure consciousness . . . pure potentiality seeking expression from the unmanifest to the manifest. . . . And when we realize that our true Self is one of pure potentiality, we align with the power that manifests everything in the universe." [21]

This book is about realizing our true self by consciously aligning our seemingly individual streams of consciousness with this ground of pure potentiality. The opportunity for transforming ourselves by joining our consciousness with this pure awareness is unlimited. In the following chapters we describe some of the ways expanded awareness appears in our lives, giving us glimpses of our unrealized potential in consciousness.

The Physics of Miracles

The Scientific Evidence for Mind-to-Mind Connections

Each human being . . . participates in an insepa-
rable way in society, and in the planet. . . . Such
participation goes on, perhaps ultimately to some
yet more comprehensive mind . . . beyond even the
human species as a whole.

— Physicist David Bohm

In a famous scene from Shakespeare's great play, Hamlet warns Horatio that "There are more things in heaven and earth . . . than are dreamt of in your philosophy." In the same spirit, there is more to our life experience than meets even the scientific eye. In the previous chapter we discussed how, for thousands of years, people have looked for ways to experience expanded consciousness. Since ancient times, transcendent awareness has been sought through the esoteric practices of Yoga, meditation, and prayer. These approaches offer opportunities to participate in the experience of oceanic communication that is available to the quiet mind. But most scientists want to be sure that the quieted mind isn't deceiving itself. This chapter takes the first steps toward presenting the data scientists need for that assurance.

Scientists find truth through data. For the mystic, and many nonscientists, experience is the data. Although we shall present evidence that psychic abilities were used to successfully spy on the

Russians during the Cold War, this is not the purpose we envision for psychic functioning. We discuss psychic abilities because they represent expanded awareness that is available to us all. These capacities are empowering; they allow us not only to realize our connection to one another but also to actively participate in the larger universe in which we live. We can have an effect in the world, even from our armchair.

Remote Viewing

What evidence exists that separation of consciousness is only an illusion? The answer comes from twenty-five hundred years of recorded experience of mystics, sages, and teachers, and a century of scientific research into extrasensory perception in the laboratory. This research includes evidence for telepathic mind-to-mind connections, clairvoyant descriptions of hidden objects and events, and precognitive experience of events that have not yet happened. Today this is called *psi* research. When we speak of consciousness in this context, we refer to our awareness of the world, as well as our awareness of our self. It is important to remember that these psychic phenomena were not invented in a laboratory but found occurring naturally in the field.

Although Buddha taught that separation is an illusion, and the great Hindu teacher Patanjali described these experiences with exquisite precision two hundred years before Christ, we know these accounts of personal experience will not convince a skeptic that psi abilities exist. In presenting the most compelling data, we will focus first on our own research into the clairvoyant perception called remote viewing. It is the ability to know and describe events and places at distant points in space and time through the application of focused attention. We have now encountered hundreds of people who have learned to describe what exists across the street, across the city, or around the planet, often with great accuracy. These results have been published in the most prestigious scientific journals in the world: *The Proceedings of the Institute of Electrical and Electronics Engineers (IEEE), Nature,* and *The Proceedings of the American Association for the Advancement of Science (AAAS).* [1]

In my (Russell's) work as cofounder of the research program at Stanford Research Institute, I investigated psi abilities for the CIA and other government agencies in the 1970s and 1980s. I spent more than ten years conducting experiments in an electrically shielded room with men and women who were able to describe in great detail the insides and outsides of buildings in the Soviet Union and elsewhere. This secret program of research and applications achieved such scientific and operational success that it was supported in its various incarnations by the U.S. government for more than twenty years. It is only through our persistence with the Freedom of Information Act that we are able to tell you of these adventures today.

In the *Sutras of Patanjali,* the great teacher was not trying to interest people in developing their psychic abilities. He was actually preparing a guide on how to know God. But the mystic knew from experience that once people learn to quiet their minds they begin to have all sorts of interesting experiences: seeing into the distance, experiencing the future, diagnosing illness, healing the sick, and much more. His goal was to help his students to achieve transcendence, not to display these powers or *siddhis.*

We are aware that few of our readers are interested in becoming mystics, fortune tellers, or psychic spies. But we perceive these abilities, and the mental interconnectedness that they imply, to be relevant to a discussion of the Perennial Philosophy. We believe they should be seen as matters of experience rather than belief. Patanjali was able to give step-by-step instructions for what might be called omniscience, and the quiet mind. He taught that to see the moon reflected in a pool of water, you must wait until every ripple is stilled. So it is with the mind. He taught that "Yoga (union with God) is

mind wave quieting" — a first step to either knowing God or transcendence. The omniscience one achieves doesn't mean we can know
everything, because we are only finite beings. But by asking one question at a time, we *can* know anything we need to know.

What do we mean by nonlocal mind? The Buddhists had it right:
Our consciousness *is* both here and not-here. Some scientists have
mistakenly explained consciousness as being created by and existing
in the brain. Consciousness is not an epi-phenomenon of brain
chemistry. It is *your* self-awareness, which we know from laboratory
experiments can have a direct and measurable telepathic effect on *my*
experience.

Nonlocal Connections

The idea of "nonlocal connections" came to the physics world's
attention in 1935, when Albert Einstein, together with Boris Podolsky
and Nathan Rosen, published a now-famous physics paper entitled,
"Can a Quantum Mechanical Description of Physical Reality Be
Considered Complete?" [2] The paper showed that, according to
Quantum Theory, photons sent off in opposite directions at the
speed of light might under certain conditions maintain a connection
with each other. Today we call these photons "entangled."

Einstein thought this correlation between photons traveling
away from each other — which he called "ghostly action-at-a-
distance" — might allow messages to be sent faster than the speed of
light. This might occur if we could make changes in a beam of photons coming toward us, and observe *reliable* corresponding changes
in another beam traveling away from us, which we can't. According
to Relativity Theory, two points that are receding from each other at
the speed of light cannot maintain an informational connection.
Einstein therefore concluded that there must be something fundamentally wrong with Quantum Theory.

Physics experiments testing Einstein's conclusion have now been carried out in several laboratories worldwide: by Stuart Freedman and John Clauser in Berkeley in 1972, by Alain Aspect and his colleagues in Paris in 1982, and most recently by Nicholas Gisin in Geneva. [3] In all these experiments, when two beams of light from the same source were simultaneously sent off in opposite directions, the photons in these light beams remained entangled even when seven miles apart.

These experiments demonstrate that widely separated photons do indeed appear to be correlated with each other — even after a person changes the angle at which the light is polarized at one end of the measuring system. However, because all the photons in the experiment fluctuate randomly, the person at the receiving end of the system observing fluctuating photons has no way to determine whether the sender did or did not change the polarization of the light at "his" end of the experiment. This is why one cannot send a message with this system. In recent weeks, this kind of entanglement — called nonlocal connection — has even been observed with atoms. [4]

Einstein was correct in his analysis showing a connection between photons receding from each other at the speed of light. At this time, however, it seems that he was mistakenly concerned that this connection violates Relativity Theory; it does not appear that the entangled photons can be used to send messages. But Einstein and his colleagues' analysis in the 1930s, together with the contemporary experiments cited above, have given scientific support to the current view of *nonlocal connectedness*. Although these correlations themselves probably do not explain mind-to-mind connections, we view them as unequivocal laboratory evidence of the nonlocality that makes these connections possible. It is likely that this evidence for our nonlocal universe will turn out to be one of the most profound things we have learned this century.

Einstein published these ideas sixty years ago, yet today's leading physicists still do not agree on all the implications of these nonlocal connections. In fact, Nobel Prize–winning physicist Brian Josephson wrote of these experiments, "The existence of such remote influences or connections is suggested [even] more directly by experiments on phenomena such as telepathy (the connection of one mind to another) and psychokinesis (the direct influence of mind on matter), both of which are examples of so-called psi functioning." [5]

Are We Connected or Separate?

In the Diamond Sutra, the Buddha tells us many confusing things, such as, "This is neither a teaching nor not a teaching." What is a poor student to do? The four-valued logic of the second-century enlightened master Nagarjuna helps us to understand the Buddhist concept that we are both here and not here. Nagarjuna taught that statements about the world can be (1) true, (2) not true, (3) both true and not true, and (4) neither true nor not true, which he felt is usually the case.

The good news is that you don't have to possess the understanding of a dharma master (enlightened teacher) to have a meaningful and spiritual life. Our knowledge is frequently neither true nor not true. In physics, for example, we discovered the important knowledge that light is neither a wave, nor not a wave. Within the time domain, we are both eternal and not eternal. And with regard to separation, we are both separate in body and united in consciousness. Rabbi Jesus was a man, an inspired teacher, and a particle of matter two thousand years ago, yet his teaching — the Christ Spirit — is a wave that transcends all space and time, and illuminates us today. David Bohm and Basil Hiley remind us in *The Undivided Universe,* that "Since there is no final theory, it cannot be said that the universe is either ultimately deterministic or ultimately indeterministic. Therefore we cannot from physical theories alone draw any conclusions, for example, about the ultimate limits of human freedom." [6]

From Theoretical Physics to Mental Connections

In recognition of Carl Sagan's admittance that some ESP phenomena deserve more research, we begin with evidence from remote viewing experiments carried out at Stanford Research Institute (SRI), which we consider the most robust of all direct perception experiments. We will then describe the dream telepathy and sensory deprivation experiments that Sagan found compelling. We will briefly explore the apparent ability of some people to affect the operation of computer-driven random number generators, and, finally, we will discuss our personal experience with precognition.

Carl Sagan now knows more than any of us about nonlocal mind — the mind that transcends space and time. But if we had ten minutes with the living Carl Sagan, we would show him the data from remote viewing research as our best evidence that consciousness in not limited to the physical body.

Simply put, our experience is that once a person, even a government scientist, has come to understand the SRI remote viewing data, they are much less likely to deny the reality of psychic abilities than they were before. These data show that people in the laboratory week after week, year after year, have described what is going on in the world at great distances from their physical body. We present this research, and how to do it, in our previous book, *Miracles of Mind.* 7

Although we do not yet have a physical mechanism to propose for remote viewing, the experiments are easy to do, and the data are often compelling. David Bohm describes this interconnectedness as a holographic universe, in which each piece is connected with each other piece. In his book *The Undivided Universe,* Bohm says of this quantum-interconnectedness, *"The essential features . . . are that the whole universe is in some way enfolded in everything, and that each thing is enfolded in the whole"* — which reiterates the Buddha's statement from direct experience that "separation is an illusion."

In 1973, the first year of the SRI research, Pat Price, a retired police commissioner from Burbank, California, contacted SRI and said that he would like to help with the remote viewing work. Price declared that he had used ESP all his life as a police commissioner to catch law-breakers by psychically scanning the city to locate where the frightened criminal was hiding. Price arrived at SRI with a scrapbook of clippings attesting to his psychic prowess. A formal series of experiments was quickly carried out, in which Pat was asked approximately once a week to describe his mental impressions of the location where one of our experimental team had been secreted somewhere in the San Francisco Bay Area.

My job was to interview Price, to help him describe the distant location, as yet unknown to either me or my colleague Hal Puthoff. This is a called a "double blind" protocol, because neither the experimenters nor the remote viewer knows anything about the day's target, or the target pool locations from which it was selected. At the end of nine trials, a similarly "blind" judge was asked to rate each of Price's descriptions and drawings as to how well they matched each of the nine targets used in the experiment. The judge, a Stanford University English professor, achieved seven out of nine first-place matches. That indicates that if someone had been kidnapped by terrorists to one of nine suspected locations on nine consecutive weeks, Price would have found them the first place he looked seven out of the nine times. The likelihood of that happening by chance is less than one in thirty thousand. Puthoff and I published these results in the March 1976 issue of *Proceedings of the IEEE.* The paper was called "A Perceptual Channel for Information Transfer over Kilometer Distances."

Because it appeared we could focus our psychic gaze anywhere we wished, we thought that we could approach the Central Intelligence Agency for possible financial support. We were concerned with the issues that arise when working with the CIA, but in the middle of the

Cold War we felt that more information was better for the world than less information. We were in favor of intelligence, as opposed to ignorance.

After talking with many staff people, our great supporter at the Agency, Dr. Kit Green, arranged for us to have an audience with the Director for Intelligence, John McMahon. John was an "old hand" from the operational side of the Agency, and was well known to not suffer fools gladly. He listened to our description of the experiments with Pat Price and other SRI remote viewers, and told us of similar experiences told to him by friends in Vietnam. McMahon concluded the interview by telling us that we were "wasting our time looking at churches and swimming pools in California." He had sites that really needed scrutinizing — ten thousand miles away in the Soviet Union.

The following week we began what was to become one of our most significant adventures. A physicist from the CIA showed up at SRI with geographical coordinates, latitude and longitude, for a Soviet target McMahon wanted us to describe. None of us, of course, knew anything about the site. This was to be a demonstration of ability test. They wanted any information we could give them, and were eager to learn if we could describe a target thousands of miles away with only coordinates from which to work. If we could describe the outside, which had been observed by satellite photography, at that time a top secret capability, we would then be asked to describe the inside.

Price and I locked ourselves into the small electrically shielded room on the second floor of SRI's Radio Physics building where we conducted our experiments, and I read Price the coordinates. He was silent for about a minute, and then began his description: "I am lying on my back on the roof of a two- or three-story brick building. It's a sunny day. The sun feels good. There's the most amazing thing. There's a giant gantry crane moving back and forth over my head. . . . As I drift up in the air and look down, it seems to be riding on a track with one rail on each side of the building. I've never seen anything like that."

Pat then sketched the layout of the buildings and the crane, which he labeled as a gantry. Several days later we completed the remote viewing exercise. We were eventually told that the site was the super-secret Soviet atomic bomb laboratory at Semipalatinsk.

The astonishing accuracy of Price's drawing compared to the CIA drawings of the Semipalatinsk facility is the sort of thing that I, as a physicist, would never have believed, if I had not seen it myself. Price went on to draw many other items at the site, most of which were confirmed. One of the most interesting things Price saw was the interior of the building on top of which he was "psychically" lying — an interior unknown to anyone in our government at the time.

He described a large room where people were assembling a giant, sixty-foot-in-diameter metal sphere from thick metal gores, like sections of an orange peel. He said they were having trouble welding it all together because the pieces were warping. Three years later we discovered just how accurate Price's viewing had been, when the sphere-fabricating activity at Semipalatinsk was described in the May 1977 issue of *Aviation Week* magazine. The account confirmed all of Price's descriptions, including the problem with the welding of the pieces. It is thought today that the Soviets were probably fabricating a particle-beam weapon designed to shoot down American spy satellites.

Our CIA contract monitor, Dr. Kenneth Kress, wrote a classified memoir describing our work for him, which was published in 1977 in the CIA journal *Studies in Intelligence*. "Tantalizing but incomplete data have been generated by CIA-sponsored research," Kress writes. "These data show, among other things, that on occasion unexplained results of genuine intelligence significance occur." [8] He quotes a second CIA operations officer who was summoned to evaluate Price's data: "It is my considered opinion that this technique — whatever it is — offers definite operational possibilities." The following year, just before his untimely death, Price worked directly for Kress at CIA headquarters.

One intriguing aspect of Price's insights into the interior of the Soviet facility was that his perception of the sixty-foot sphere and "gores" was made without any feedback at all. We had originally expected feedback to be an important ingredient of remote viewing. But Price was not reading the mind of the sponsor, because no one in the United States knew of the sphere. Nor could Pat have been pre-cognitively looking at his own feedback from the future, because he died in 1975, before the details of the sphere were independently con-firmed. His remarkable perception was a *direct experience* of the site.

In 1979, after a formal Congressional investigation, Congressman Charles Rose said of this experiment in *Omni* magazine: "All I can say is that if the results were faked, our security system doesn't work. What these people 'saw' was confirmed by aerial photography. There is no way it could have been faked."

Even a Scientist Can Be Psychic

We must close our eyes and invoke a new manner of seeing. . .
a wakefulness that is the birthright of us all,
though few put it to use.
— Plotinus (seventeen centuries ago)

The year after Pat died we received a call from another man with extraordinary psychic ability. This time it was a creative young research physicist named Gary Langford who was working in the Intelligence Analysis group at SRI. He had been following our work, and thought that he could help us, because he, like Price, had been doing distant viewing for years. He told us that he first experienced psychic functioning as a child. He was not a great baseball player, but his precognitive ability told him where to stand in the outfield to catch fly balls that would come his way.

Gary's job at SRI was to read translations of Russian technology reports, look at photos of the U.S.S.R., and try to figure out what the Soviets were doing. Often when he was given a typical poor-quality photograph taken from a great altitude, he would have the experience of looking intently, and then saying something like, "It looks like a submarine off the coast." To which the others would respond incredulously, "Where the hell do you see a submarine?" And that was a problem, because there wasn't really any sub to be seen. It would frequently turn out, however, that his intuition was remarkably correct.

Gary, Pat, and many others seem to be able to move their perceptual point of view at a target. They are able to experience the target location as if they were actually there. These experienced viewers are able to psychically move around the site and relate what they see.

Gary participated in the SRI program for more than a decade. Like many viewers, his *accuracy* in describing details was excellent at the start and did not improve greatly. What did improve was his *reliability* — he became correct more often. And he became increasingly able to tell when he had made really strong contact with the target he was trying to describe. When he had "that special feeling," he was almost always correct. That type of self-awareness is extremely desirable in a remote viewer. Sometimes, he did not have a confident feeling, but he gave an accurate description nonetheless. It's remarkable that we can be correct two-thirds of the time, but we are still baffled at being wrong at all.

Gary joined us as a regular viewer as we began to investigate the accuracy of remote viewing at increasing distances. We wanted to know if remote viewing accuracy would fall off like television reception does when you move too far from the transmitter. Would the mental pictures become snowy? One of Gary's first tasks was to follow me as I traveled across the U.S. as an outbound beacon. He had no idea of my itinerary.

My first stop was New Orleans, to carry out remote viewing trials with a friend in medical school at Tulane University. We bought a picture book of New Orleans sites of interest, and threw a die on the pavement to determine which of six possible targets I would visit for the trial. The target that came up was the Louisiana Superdome sports arena. Gary's interviewer for this trial was Dr. Elizabeth Rauscher, a physics professor at the University of California, Berkeley. She and I had already worked together for several years trying to develop a physical model for psi functioning. Elizabeth was an experienced interviewer, and sensitive to the nuances of the remote viewing process.

At the moment I walked toward the Superdome, Elizabeth was building rapport with Gary in the shielded room at SRI. At noon, I came upon the glistening building. I was shocked by the size of it, and said into my tape recorder, "This is a remote viewing experiment with Russ Targ and Gary Langford. I am at the 80,000 seat New Orleans Superdome. It is a metal-sided building that looks like nothing so much as a great flying saucer shining in the noon day sun."

Meanwhile, back in the Menlo Park laboratory, Gary was just beginning his description for Elizabeth. "I've got a problem," he said. "All I see is a damn UFO in the middle of a city!" Elizabeth, the intrepid interviewer, told him, "That's okay, Gary. Why don't you just take a break, and then make a drawing of what you are looking at." This is what we called "debriefing the initial images." Gary then made the remarkable drawings shown in the illustration. He said he saw, "a large circular building with a white dome." He went on to describe "glass cases around the inside," which we later verified as true, even though I did not have access to the inside of the building at the time.

His ability to describe details beyond what was available to us in feedback photos was truly amazing. It is clear that he had contact with the target, and was not reading my mind, psychically looking over my shoulder, or observing his feedback pictures. The

Superdome photo and Gary's drawings are both shown below. Gary described a concrete path around the building, on which he correctly showed me walking; he also drew the many ramps leading up into the building.

 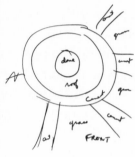

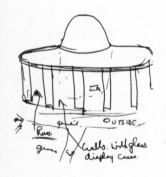 

LONG DISTANCE REMOTE VIEWING EXPERIMENT — SRI Menlo Park to Louisiana Superdome. Subject described circular building with a white dome. 31 October 1976.

Gary has now been doing remote viewing for almost twenty years. From the hundreds of trials he has completed, it appears that he achieves this kind of accuracy about 25 percent of the time. Our work with him and others has shown that remote viewing accuracy is not at all affected by distance and the first glimpses are the most reliable.

Miracles with Army Intelligence

During the summer of 1979, my colleague Hal and I conducted remote viewing experiments with six inexperienced military men from Fort Mead. We selected the viewers who would be the most likely candidates for remote viewing from among a group of thirty men by interviewing them about their life experiences and their thoughts and beliefs about ESP. We were especially looking for men who had profound ESP experiences in the course of their lives and work. Most of these men wish to remain anonymous, but one of them, Joe McMoneagle, has written a thoughtful book entitled *Mind Trek,* describing his introduction to remote viewing at SRI, and his psychic adventures since leaving.

Joe is an affable, energetic, fullback of a man. He always seemed to me to be ready to burst off running out of his leather jacket. You wouldn't have known from looking at him that ten years before, he had had a near-death experience in Germany. As he was leaving a bar, he became ill, passed out, fell to the cobblestones, and as he explained it, "was received by God." He felt embraced by a powerful light, and was delivered to the hospital with no pulse at all. But he told us that was okay with him because he was saying to himself, "So this is what God is like!" This transforming experience was his introduction and opening to a whole world of psychic awareness. The story of how he began to integrate his psychic experiences is truly extraordinary. (Let us assure you that we consider a near-death experience to be an unnecessarily high price to pay for psychic development!)

A few weeks after our interviews, I was sitting with Joe in our remote viewing lab in California. I explained that all we wanted him to do was describe his mental pictures of our researcher's location. I told him I had no idea where that might be, but if he would like to make some little sketches of what he saw in his mind's eye, that these

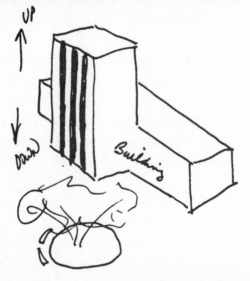

Stanford Art Museum Target (a), and Response (b), by Viewer Joe McMoneagle in 1979.

often match the place where the researchers are hiding. It also turned out that he had much better than average drawing skills.

When the time came for Joe to do his first trial, he saw a number of shapes: a teepee, a barbell, a piano keyboard, and a building, all of which he drew around the edge of a piece of paper. Joe says in his book, "I actually began to feel like I was more at my imaginary building than in the room talking with Russell Targ." I asked Joe to pull away from the building and describe its general shape. He said, "It's like an inverted rectangle with a square fastened to the back of it, or a rectangle laid down behind it. It's like two buildings in one." [9]

After the interview, Joe made the detailed drawing we show in the figure. In the upper part of the picture you can see Joe's rendering of what he called the "keyboard effect," together with a planter in front of the building. He clearly shows the tall pillared-front of a building, with the lower extensions to the left and right. The lower part of the figure is a photograph of the Stanford University Art Museum, where the researchers had been sent by their random number generator. Joe was a natural. Needless to say, the judges had no trouble matching his drawings with the Art Museum when they visited it, even though there were many small unrelated sketches around the edges of the page.

Joe went on to complete a highly successful series of trials with us, and he was able to greatly improve his accuracy, even over this very good sketch. My associates and I proceeded to work with five other men who showed us that psi abilities come in all sizes and shapes of people.

The overall results from the formal judging of this study were highly significant. Four of the six government viewers each produced statistically meaningful results — a highly improbable result, with odds of greater than one in ten thousand. All of them went on to teach many others in the U.S. Armed Services how to successfully perform remote viewing. In 1984 Joe was granted a National Legion of Merit Award for excellence in his military intelligence career, including his operational remote viewing.

By the end of the first decade of such research, twenty-eight experimental series had been published from several labs worldwide. In an analysis of these papers, it was found that more than half, (fifteen out of twenty-eight) showed statistically significant results, where only one in twenty would be expected to reach significance by chance.[10] In our work at SRI, we found that a viewer would, in general, give descriptions of distant geographical locations that could be successfully matched first place by a judge in four out of six trials. Such a hit rate gives a statistically significant result, and is extraordinarily high compared with usual laboratory experience in ESP testing.

Telepathy in Our Dreams

Psychic dreams have been with us since the days of Cassandra in ancient Greece, and Joseph and Pharaoh in the Old Testament. From the data collected by parapsychologist Louisa Rhine, it appears that more than half of all spontaneous ESP experiences take place in dreams.[11] Sigmund Freud wrote about the telepathic content of dreams,[12] and in *Parapsychology and the Unconscious,* psychiatrist Jule Eisenbud has written about patients who have dreamed of events in Eisenbud's own life.[13]

Dramatic stories of telepathic dreams abound: Toward the end of World War II, several prisoners made a daring escape from the Sobibor concentration camp. One of the survivors of this courageous break is Esther Robb, who described a dream she had the night before the escape in a 1998 National Public Radio interview:

In her dream, her deceased mother was urging her to press on to reach a strange-looking barn. The next day, the twenty-year-old Esther successfully escaped the camp, climbed the fence, and walked over the bodies of people who had already fallen on mines outside the barrier. Traveling with serious wounds, she survived days of starvation and hiding in the woods. She finally saw a wooden structure far in the distance, and realized that it was the barn that her mother had shown her in her dream.

When darkness came, she managed to sneak into the barn and climb into its hay loft. As she reached the top step of the ladder, a strong hand grabbed her ankle, and called out for her to stop. It was the hand of her brother, who had just escaped from a different camp, and had found his way to the same barn.

Based on the idea that dreams might hold reliable ESP information, in the 1960s researchers at Maimonides Hospital in Brooklyn, New York, undertook a decade-long study of psychic events in dreams. This pioneering team included psychiatrist Dr. Montague Ullman, the hospital's research director, psychologist Stanley Krippner, and writer and researcher Alan Vaughan. The team performed many innovative experiments in which a subject was asked to go to sleep and dream about a randomly chosen painting that a sender would be looking at throughout the night. The researchers attached electrodes to the subjects' heads to determine from brain waves and rapid eye movements (R.E.M.) when they had entered dreaming sleep.

In the Maimonides experiments the researchers would, at the first signs of R.E.M. activity, alert the sender — who sat ninety-eight feet away in another part of the hospital — to pay particular attention to the picture he or she was sending. At the end of each dream period throughout the night, the experimenters would awaken the subject and ask them to describe their dreams.

The results were remarkable. In series after series, which they describe in their book *Dream Telepathy,* the sleeper was able to relate dream experiences that were strongly correlated with the pictures that the sender was looking at. [14] These statistically significant correlations were made by "blind" judges who had to match each of the eight dream reports against eight pictures used in the experiments.

Two series of particularly successful trials were carried out with psychologist William Erwin as the sleeping subject. "Multi-sensory" materials were given to the sender to help him or her empathize with and experience the picture that they were to send. For example, when the target picture was Katz's *Interior of a Synagogue,* the multisensory materials for the sender's environment included candles like those in the painting, a candleholder, matches, and a button with Hebrew writing. In Erwin's first dream he described "something about school." In his second dream he found himself a small boy in a little town. Summing up his dreams, Erwin said: "Some kind of impression of school . . . going to school. . . . The building that I was speaking of — I spent a little time with the boy in it . . . It could have been an experience that Sol (the sender) had because he was sort of exploring. . . . During one of the studies he talked something about a synagogue. Maybe it was the one where he was dealing with the Yellow Rabbi." [15]

Specific mention of "synagogue" and "Rabbi" were enough to give this picture the highest rating in the group. The results of this study were significant at one thousand to one odds when evaluated by outside judges, who were successfully able to match each of the eight dream descriptions with the correct picture.

These experiments were important to psi research for two reasons. First, they were successful year after year for a decade, giving researchers a stable phenomenon to investigate. Even more important, this approach provided a valuable insight into the pictorial and nonanalytic processes underlying psi functioning. In the 1960s, researchers considered psi to be a weak perceptual ability, often masked by internal and external mental and somatic sensory noise. These experiments led researchers to ask, "Can we find a way to let subjects rest in a dream-like state, but still be awake enough to tell us what they are experiencing?"

Telepathy in a Controlled Environment

The *ganzfeld*, meaning "whole field," is a controlled environment used in ESP research in which all ordinary inputs to the psi subject are limited by sensory isolation. The ganzfeld idea appeared in the 1960s, when it was thought that altered states of consciousness would lead to more effective psychic functioning. The receiving person is located in a sound-proof room, with a uniform and featureless visual field. This is simply accomplished by taping Ping-Pong ball halves over the viewer's eyes and bathing them in uniform red light, while playing "white" noise through earphones.

Like the dream telepathy experiments, the ganzfeld studies investigated telepathic communication between a sender person and a receiver person. For more than fifteen years, this approach was pioneered by Dr. Charles Honorton, who was Dr. Stanley Krippner's successor at the Maimonides Hospital Research Center. In 1994, Honorton coauthored a fifteen-page paper with psychologist Dr. Daryl Bem, a professor from Cornell University and a former skeptic. With its appearance in the mainstream *Psychological Bulletin,* the article signified a landmark accomplishment in the field of psi research. [16] The paper described a series of experiments that were called "The Auto-Ganzfeld" because the researcher, sender, and receiver were all isolated from each other, and the researcher was isolated from the selection of the target video tapes, which were chosen and shown to the viewer automatically by a computer.

In these experiments, the receiver was generally a volunteer from the community whose task was to remain awake, and to describe into a tape recorder all the impressions that passed through his or her mind during a thirty-minute session. Meanwhile, the sender would view a randomly chosen video tape that played repeatedly throughout the session.

At the end of each trial, the computer controlling the experiment would show the receiver the chosen segment and three other video segments, in random order. The receiver's task was then to decide which of the four mini-movies the sender had been watching. By chance, one would expect a one-out-of-four success rate in this process. In the entire series of eleven experiments, which involved 240 people in 354 sessions, the hit rate was one out of three correct, which departs from chance expectation by 500 to 1. More important, in some of these trials, the receiver's narration was so accurate that it sounded as if the viewer were watching the target video tape right next to the sender!

We often compare psi to musical ability: it is widely distributed in the population, with everyone enjoying some aptitude —as even the most nonmusical person can learn to play a little Mozart on the piano. On the other hand, there is no substitute for innate talent or practice.

In our society, psychic functioning is to some extent forbidden, or considered evidence of mental illness. The ganzfeld ritual of securing the Ping-Pong balls over your eyes, turning on the red lights and white noise in the earphones, and slamming the heavy door of the electrically shielded, sound-proof booth has a powerful permission-giving effect on the viewer.

A large, recent ganzfeld series conducted at the Rhine Research Center in Durham, North Carolina, with more than two hundred trials, found that almost all the psi in the experiment was contributed by pairs of people who were either parents and children, or siblings. The thirty trials with these two groups of blood relations achieved an average 50 percent hit rate, where only 25 percent would be expected by chance. The siblings were by far the strongest group in the study, while married couples scored below chance expectation. An additional subclass of people were independently significant: left-handers, who scored a 45 percent hit rate. Researchers conjecture that left-handed people have more connections between the left and right brain hemispheres, which might give the analytical part of the brain access to the nonanalytic pictures and emotions experienced as a result of the ganzfeld stimulus. [17]

Viewing the Future (Precognition)

Nonlocality includes both time and space. The data from remote viewing provides evidence that our minds have access to events occurring both in distant places *and* in the future. We have a fundamental problem when writing about time because no one knows how to measure it. Rulers measure distance but clocks do not measure time; they simply tick at the rate of one tick per second. Time is a mental construct and cannot be measured by scientific instruments.

It has often been said that time was invented by God so that everything wouldn't happen at once. *A Course In Miracles* teaches that we invented time ourselves. In modern physics, time is simply seen as the "distance" between events that occur at the same place.

Precognitive dreams are probably the most common psychic event in the life of the average person. These dreams give us a glimpse of events that we will experience the next day or in the near future. In fact, we believe that the precognitive dream is *caused* by the experience that we actually will have at a later time.

If you dream of a very large black automobile passing in front of your window, and wake up the next morning and see a hearse leading a funeral procession driving down your street, we would say that last night's dream was caused by your experience of seeing the hearse the next morning. This is an example of the future affecting the past, much like the feedback in remote viewing. There is strong evidence for this kind of occurrence, which we discuss at the end of this chapter. However, it appears impossible for a future event to change the known or already-experienced past.

Nothing in the future can prevent something that has already happened. This is the so-called "intervention paradox," illustrated by the example in which you, in the present, kill your grandmother when she was a child, and you therefore cease to exist. While this is interesting to think about, there is not a drop of evidence to make us think it can occur.

To know that a dream is precognitive, you have to recognize that it is not caused by the previous day's mental residue, your wishes or anxieties. We find that precognitive dreams have an unusual clarity, but often contain bizarre and unfamiliar material. Dream experts speak of "preternatural clarity," which transcends wish fulfillment or anxiety. For example, if you are unprepared for an exam, and dream about failing it, we would not consider that to be precognition. On the other hand, if you have taken hundreds of plane flights, and then experience a frightening dream about a crash, you might reconsider your travel plans.

You might ask, "How can I dream about being in a plane crash, if I don't actually get to experience it?" The answer may be that you dream about the real crash, and then dramatize the events to include yourself in it. In one true case, a good friend dreamed about being in a plane crash, and then saw a plane crash at close range the next day. Since he was supposed to have been on that very plane, he had no trouble putting himself on the plane in his dream the previous night. We would say that the frightening crash he experienced was the cause of his earlier dream. This is called retro-causality, and it may be the basis of most precognition. There is obviously no law against pre-cognition, since under the right conditions, it is a common occur-rence, and hundreds of laboratory experiments show that it appears to work exactly as well as real-time ESP.

It's About Time

In a summary of research data from 1935 to 1989 for what we call paranormal foreknowledge of the future, researchers Charles Honorton and Diane Ferari described 309 precognition experiments using ESP test cards with five different symbols. The experiments were carried out by sixty-two different investigators involving more than fifty thousand participants in more than two million trials.[18] The percipients had to use their intuitive abilities to determine which randomly selected symbol from five potential choices they would be shown later on. In these experiments, the target picture was not even determined at the time of their intuitive guessing.

Thirty percent of these studies were statistically significant in showing that people can describe future events, where only five percent would be expected by chance. This gave overall significance of greater than 10^{20} (100 billion billion) to one, which is statistically akin to throwing seventy pennies in the air and having every one come down heads. This body of data offers very strong evidence for confirming the existence of foreknowledge of the future. Clearly, we have *some* contact with the future. This connection shows unequivocally that we misunderstand our relationship to the dimension of time we take so much for granted.

The authors have personally conducted experimental series in which people have described and experienced events that didn't occur until two or three days in the future. One of these involved precognitive forecasting of changes in the silver commodity market without actually making any trades. The authors were successful in eleven out of twelve individual calls. This is one reason we have no doubt that the precognitive channel is available.[19]

We know from the experimental psi data that a viewer in the laboratory, by focusing his or her attention, can reliably describe any location on the planet. We know, also, that this same viewer is not bound by present time. Dean Radin's comprehensive book *The Conscious Universe* discusses the published research investigating ESP in dreams. Between 1966 and 1973, 450 dream telepathy sessions were reported, with an overall score of 63 percent correct. When analyzed statistically as a group, the dreamers dreamed of the picture they were shown at a later time at a success rate of odds greater than a million to one. [20]

The familiar "river of time" model renders precognition less magical. On the average, we know that rivers flow downstream; that is, causes come before events. If we look closely at the fine structure of the stream, however, we will recognize eddies in its flow. A boulder may create a wake downstream, with the cause clearly coming before the effect. But upstream we may find a great whirlpool that comes, of course, from the boulder downstream. We may experience the effect before we see its cause. An effect preceding its cause is called retro-causality, and from the data, we believe that it is not such a rare occurrence.

Feeling the Future

We are all familiar with the idea of premonition, in which one has inner knowledge of something to happen in the future — usually something bad! There is also the experience of presentiment, where one has an inner sensation, a gut feeling, that something strange is about to occur. An example would be for you to suddenly stop on your walk down the street, because you felt "uneasy," only to have a flower pot then fall off a window ledge and land at your feet — instead of on your head. That would be a useful presentiment.

In the laboratory, we know that showing a frightening picture to a person produces a significant change in his or her physiology. Their blood pressure, heart rate, and skin resistance all change. This fight-or-flight reaction is called an "orienting response." Researcher Dean Radin has recently shown at the University of Nevada that this orienting response is also observed in a person's physiology a few seconds *before* viewing the scary picture!

In balanced, double-blind experiments, Radin has shown that just before viewing scenes of violence, your body steels itself against the insult, but that no strong anticipatory reaction precedes viewing a picture of a flower garden. Of course, fear is much easier to measure physiologically than bliss. Here, it seems, your direct physical perception of the picture, when it occurs, causes you to have a unique, *earlier* physical response. Your future is affecting your past. These experiments are also described in Radin's previously mentioned book, *The Conscious Universe.*

So Can the Future Affect the Past?

Similar experiments were carried out by Helmut Schmidt at the Mind Science Foundation in Austin, Texas. Schmidt examined the behavior of electronic random-number generators that produce long, haphazard strings of 1s and 0s.[21] He had already shown through a lifetime of work that a person could mentally interact with the machine from a distance, apparently by psi, to obtain more 1s or 0s just by paying attention to the desired outcome. In his latest and most remarkable experiments, he has shown that even *after* the machine has generated a tape recording of its output of 1s and 0s, a person can still affect the outcome by paying attention to the tape, so long as no one has seen the data beforehand. We could call this retro-psychokinesis or retro-PK.

Psychokinesis on the Internet

Presently, in 1998, a retro-PK website on the Internet has collected trials from thousands of people, and is presently showing 2.5 standard deviations from chance expectation, which corresponds to odds of about one in five hundred. We do not believe the person is actually changing the tape, which may be a punched-hole paper tape. Rather, Schmidt and others believe the person with the tape in his hand is reaching back in time to affect the machine at the time of its operation. Schmidt has even demonstrated that the prerecorded but unobserved breathing rate of a person in the past can be affected by the mental activity of a person at a later time! [22]

Similar experiments have been carried out in the Princeton Anomalies Research Laboratory. Over a period of many years, these researchers have shown that individuals can change the distribution of 1s and 0s produced by their random-number generator. But one of their most interesting findings is that pairs of people working together obtain improved performance over people working by themselves. And, most significant, so-called "bonded pairs" (boyfriend/girlfriend and the like) working together with coherent intentions, produced by far the greatest effect in changing the output of the machine.

Journeys Out of the Body

One teaching common to many spiritual thought systems is that if we visualize ourselves and our world as affirmative and loving then we experience an affirmative and loving world. This is sometimes interpreted to mean that our thoughts themselves affect the physical world — that our minds can reach beyond the body.

A striking example of this idea was an investigation of out-of-body experiences (OOBES) conducted by Karlis Osis and Donna McKormick in 1980, when Osis was director of research at the American Society for Psychical Research (ASPR). We have already described laboratory remote viewing. But a continuum exists from ordinary remote viewing, in which a person sees a distant landscape mentally, to an out-of-body experience in which a person can take to this distant place all of his or her sensitivity, emotion, even sexuality. The person is then in a position to have a full range of experiences at that location. This is described in detail in Robert Monroe's book *Journeys Out of the Body.*

In the ASPR experiments, an experienced OOBE practitioner, Alex Tanous, was asked to describe various objects Osis had arranged on a little shelf in a sealed box. This box was an electrically shielded container, which also contained a sensitive set of strain gauges that generate an electrical signal when perturbed or moved in any way. Tanous described many of the target arrangements successfully. Osis found in examining the data from the strain gauge that the largest electrical signals were generated when Tanous was giving the most accurate descriptions of the targets in the box.[23] This is not something we have ever been able to observe with ordinary remote viewing. But it strongly supports Tanous's claim that he experiences warmth, tactile sensations, and vision when he travels to a distant location. It is a full-body experience for him, not just a change in point of view.

Blind People "See" in Near-Death Experiences

These data correlate strongly with reports from those who have had near-death experiences (NDEs). Researcher Dr. Kenneth Ring describes reports from blind people who have had NDEs during which they apparently "see" with eyeless vision. They accurately describe the surroundings, people, and activities taking place in the vicinity of their comatose body as it is lying on the ground, or on a hospital operating table during their trauma.[24]

Such experiences are often accompanied by a life review, and profound experiences of loving and *being* love, which have life-changing effects on survivors. For us, the data from both OOBE experiments and NDE survivors strongly supports the idea of a self-aware consciousness separate from the physical body.

Precognition in the Lab

For years, parapsychologists have been trying to find ways to encourage their subjects to receive psychic glimpses of the future. Earlier in this chapter we mentioned a large retrospective analysis of 309 precognition experiments carried out over 50 years between 1935 and 1987. There is overwhelming evidence for the existence of precognition, but more importantly we have learned more successful and less successful ways to do experiments. Four different factors were found to vary significantly with success or failure. It is important to keep these ingredients in mind, if you want your own psi experiments to succeed.

Experiments are much more successful when they are carried out with subjects who are experienced and interested in the outcome. For example, running ESP experiments in a whole classroom of moderately bored students will rarely show any kind of ESP success. Participants who are enthusiastic about the experiment are the most successful in these precognition studies. The difference in scoring between these two kinds of tests, with experienced and inexperienced subjects, was significant at 1000 to 1 against chance.

The most comprehensive laboratory examination of precognition was performed by Dr. Robert Jahn, Brenda Dunne, and Dr. Roger Nelson at Princeton University. [25] They conducted 227 formal experiments in which a viewer was asked to describe where one of the researchers would be hiding at some preselected later time. They discovered, much to their surprise, that the accuracy of the description was the same whether the viewer had to look hours, days, or weeks into the future. As judges compared descriptions with target locations, the overall statistical significance of the combined experiments departed from what you would expect from chance by a probability of one in a hundred billion!

It is difficult to read about their work and not be convinced of the reality of precognition, even though we don't understand how it works. The most important finding of the combined data — from dozens of such precognition experiments from many laboratories throughout the world — is that it is *no harder to psychically see the future than it is to psychically see hidden events in the present.* This is the mystery that captivates us.

Eternity and Timelessness

The great significance of this work does not come from statistics. What is exciting is that these findings strongly reinforce the idea of our connectivity through time as well as space. They demonstrate that we are more than bodies, and that our minds have no boundaries, just as the Perennial Philosophy teaches.

In the next chapter we discuss the evidence that some aspect of our personality survives bodily death. We end this section with the words of philosopher Ludwig Wittgenstein, who reminds us with his usual precision of the difference between eternity and timelessness. In the *Tractatus* he writes: "If we take eternity to mean not infinite temporal duration, but timelessness, then eternal life belongs to those who live in the present. Our life has no end in just the same way in which our visual field has no limits." [26] Maybe this is the same thing Indian sage Ramana Maharshi meant when he said, "The real Self is continuous and unaffected. . . . " [27]

CHAPTER

4

What Survives?

An Empirical Look at Life after Death

We now have, for the first time in the history of our species, compelling empirical evidence for belief in some form of personal survival after death.
— Robert Almeder, Ph.D., professor of philosophy, Georgia State University

Today, at the end of the prosperous twentieth century, ironically, many find the search for meaning in their lives becoming even more urgent than the search for financial security. For example, psychiatrist Eric Fromm has said that his distressed patients were really suffering from "an inner deadness. They live in the midst of plenty and are joyless."

Most of us, although we may avoid asking it aloud, at one time or another wonder, "Do we live out our lives, and then vanish like a bubble, leaving not a trace?" This enduring question is directly related to our search for meaning and our passion to discover who we really are.

In the 1870s, at the height of his fame, Leo Tolstoy seriously contemplated suicide. Although he had just completed *Anna Karenina* to great critical acclaim, he felt overcome with the meaningless of life. In his *Confessions* he wrote, "I felt a horror of what awaited me. . . . I could not patiently await the end . . . and I longed to free myself. . . . by a rope or a pistol ball." [1]

As Sylvia Cranston and Carey Williams describe in their book *Reincarnation,* Tolstoy in desperation began to address the question of "Who am I?" [2] He concluded that he was "a part of the infinite" and that "in these few words lies the whole problem." Tolstoy went on to create a new personal philosophy of love, simplicity, and non-violence, gratefully resuming his productive life.

In the previous chapter we described the many ways in which our conscious selves can experience oneness with the infinite nonlocal universe. In this chapter we present research data suggesting that a subconscious part of ourselves has a similar connection — a part, as you are doubtless aware, often called our spirit or soul.

Communications from the Dead

While Tolstoy was considering ending his life over his sense of separation, a group of English scientists and philosophers at Cambridge University in 1882 were forming the Society for Psychical Research (SPR). One of the leaders of this group was the classicist and poet Frederic W.H. Myers. In the introduction to his monumental, thirteen-hundred-page *Human Personality and Its Survival of Bodily Death,* Myers writes, "In the long story of man's endeavors to understand his own environment . . . there is one gap or omission so singular that its simple statement has the air of a paradox. Yet it is strictly true to say that man has never yet applied the methods of modern science to the problem which most profoundly concerns him — whether or not his personality involves any elements which survive bodily death." [3]

In the one hundred years since Myers wrote these words, modern science has answered his plea and applied itself to the meticulous compilation of thousands of mediumistic communications, apparitions of the recently dead, out-of-body experiences, and children's memories of previous lives. These data, when taken together, provide the answer Myers was seeking. And the answer is that it is *more reasonable* to believe that some aspect of our personality survives than to assert the opposite. We are not arguing that the case for survival is proven — rather, the case is strong enough for a reasonable person to feel comfortable holding that position.

It is important to note that the British SPR was not at all predisposed to conclude that the spiritualists and mediums of Victorian London were actually communicating with the dead. In fact, the membership of the SPR included the greatest debunkers of their day — perhaps of any day. Myers, himself, was concerned with two types of data being observed: first, the phenomenon of apparitions appearing at the moment of death, which he saw as "testifying to supersensory communication between the dying man and his friend who sees him." Second, he studied apparitions of people who had recently died but were seen by a friend sometime *after* the death. These appeared even in cases where the deaths "were yet unknown to the percipient, and were thus not due to mere brooding memory, but rather due to the continued action of the departing spirit." [4]

The unspoken question in these cases is whether the information of the death comes from the spirit of the deceased person, from some sort of ESP by the percipient, or from some interaction between the two. This question was particularly relevant to the society's study of séances, in which a person known as a medium would put him- or herself into an altered state of consciousness for the purpose of communicating with the dead.

The SPR members attempted to rule out the possibility of fraud or trickery on the part of the mediums, as well as mere telepathic communication between the medium and the sitters attending the seance. They found that the stream of often intimate information provided to anonymous sitters made deception extremely unlikely.

The society's experiences with mediums were often quite striking. These psychically sensitive people would enter a trance and allow themselves to become a channel for information either about the sitters present, or the sitters' loved ones who had recently died. For example, an investigator would attend a séance, and the medium in her trance would proceed to describe personal details about the investigator's dead family members — information known only by the investigator himself or by some deceased relative. The investigators were always concerned, however, that the medium might be telepathically receiving information from some living person, even in cases where no knowledgeable person was present.

More recently, psychical researcher Scott Rogo related a case from Myers' journal, discussed in the 1927 proceedings of the Society for Psychical Research, in which all knowledgeable parties had long since passed away, and yet the psychic information reappeared. In his book *Parapsychology: A Century of Inquiry,* Rogo describes the 1921 death of a man named Chaffin, a farmer in North Carolina. 5 Chaffin wrote his will in 1905, leaving all his money and property to his third son, Marshall, and disinheriting his other two sons and wife. Four years after Chaffin Sr.'s death, one of the other sons, James, had vivid visions of his father during a night of restless sleep. The apparition kept repeating, "You will find my will in my overcoat pocket."

James found the overcoat in the possession of another brother. Together, they felt a paper sewn inside the lining of the coat. Ripping out the lining, they found a note that read, "Read the twenty-seventh chapter of Genesis in my daddy's old bible." The bible, still in their mother's possession, cracked and fell into three pieces when opened. It revealed a will dated 1919, dividing the property equally. Because the handwriting was clearly that of Chaffin Sr., the will was never contested.

This case is unlikely to be either telepathic or fraudulent, because no living person knew the location of the will. The concern of the day was whether it was James's own clairvoyant ability that enabled him to find the will, even though it had never been spoken of. This "super-psi" hypothesis has been one of the most contentious topics of psi research for the past hundred years. Another, more contemporary, case that presents the "super-psi" possibility concerns the last woman to be jailed for witchcraft in Britain in 1944. A recent Reuters news account related this case in which virtually all knowledgeable parties were deceased, but the information appeared nonetheless.

The Last English Witch

During World War II, an English medium was imprisoned for witchcraft after her psychic conversation with a drowned English sailor. This true story is important because it shows how powerful personal needs are often the guiding force behind spontaneous psychic occurrences.

The medium, Helen Duncan, was conducting a séance for a group of English women in Birmingham when she was contacted by the spirit of a recently deceased man. The man claimed to be a sailor from the H.M.S. *Barham,* which he said had just been sunk by the Germans. He wanted to talk with his mother, who was in the audience, and told her through the medium that everyone had drowned, including himself.

The story of the séance and the *Barham* quickly reached British Naval Intelligence, who immediately arrested the woman, since the events she recounted were true but classified. The government authorities very much wanted to conceal such sinkings from the public to bolster wartime morale. Mrs. Duncan was taken to the dreaded Old Bailey prison at London Bridge, where she was convicted of practicing witchcraft. Prime Minister Winston Churchill, who was sympathetic to psychic phenomena, interceded on her behalf, but without success. The government argued the woman was a witch, a menace to national security, and a threat to the government's code-breaking activities.

Mrs. Duncan remained in prison for the duration of the war. Churchill was so outraged by this injustice that he personally saw to the repeal of England's 1735 Witchcraft Act. Churchill's efforts enabled witchcraft to become recognized as a bona fide religion, with witches enjoying the same privileges as ministers and clergy. According to a January 1998 Reuters story, a posthumous pardon for Mrs. Duncan is now in the works, forty years after her death. [6]

The case shows that we don't have to return to the nineteenth century to find accurate mediums. The "super-psi" hypothesis would claim that Mrs. Duncan's own clairvoyant ability, without the help of any discarnate spirit, allowed her to access the secret information. However, the "super-psi" explanation does not adequately address the issue of the importance of the message. The dead son's loving connection with his mother, creating an ostensible need for him to communicate "from the other side," is an important element in this and similar cases. This well-documented incident demonstrates the ability of our minds to function in nonlocal realms, accessing information unavailable through any ordinary channel.

Since we know from data presented in the previous chapter that people can draw upon almost omniscient perceptions, how can we tell if a message comes directly from the dead, or simply from the medium's nonlocal awareness? One approach to this vexing problem is to send a "surrogate sitter" to the medium. Thus, if I wanted to learn about my deceased grandmother Esther, I would send a friend who had never known anything about her to sit with the medium. My friend would appear anonymously and ask for information about Esther. In this case the sitter would have absolutely nothing to contribute to the session. Mysteriously, these so called "proxy sittings" have been found in every way to be as successful as the ordinary sittings. In both cases, the direct clairvoyance of the medium is still a conceivable channel for the information.

One notable "proxy sitting" was with the famous Boston medium Mrs. Leonora Piper. Researchers — including the American philosopher and psychologist William James, then at Harvard University — studied Mrs. Piper for more than twenty-five years. James sent twenty-five of his friends to visit Mrs. Piper anonymously, and instructed them to send him the names and other facts she produced.

The following case involving Mrs. Piper is reported by William James and is included in Myers' book. It has the spontaneity of a long-distance phone conversation, except that the conversation is with the deceased. A woman at the medium's sitting is reminiscing with her brother's dead friend about adventures the two men shared years before. Her brother was absent but still living, and the stories were unknown to the sister, or anyone else in the room. Myers writes:

> . . . Miss Warner had her two sittings January 6th and 7th, 1897. She remarked to me that (the spirit communicator) Hart knew one of her brothers, Charlie, and they went to the Azores together. She knew nothing about the trip except that they had watched their ship break up on the rocks.
>
> [For Hart] "I am here. Tell her that I see her, and I long to ask her brother if he recalls the storm we experienced."
>
> (I know he does. I have heard him speak of it.)
>
> "Good, and ask him if he still has a stick like mine. Take the pipe old chap, I don't wish it." [Some confusion as to which of the sitters he is talking to.]
>
> Hart continues: "We went to a queer little hotel, at a little hotel together. Charlie had a headache from hunger. We were almost starved when we got there. The food was bad, the food was bad, poor. . . . I am content here. Do you ever see me as I really am?"
>
> (No. I don't see you at all. . . . Tell some more.)
>
> "We went up to the hotel, and ask him if he recalls the laugh we had after we got up to our room. Give him my love."

(What did you laugh about?)

"Because of the dirt etc. . . . very amusing, give Charles my love, and don't forget about the stick."

Myers continues:

Charley Warner (her brother) had gone to California, and in reply to inquiries he wrote February 2nd, 1897: "J.H. and myself, once were hove to on the North Atlantic, for about three days during a severe storm. At another time we were at Horta, Royal Island, and watched our vessel drag ashore and break up, on account of a very bad storm. J.H. had a very serviceable stick. As I remember it, a stout little blade dropped out of the ferrule. I never had one like it that I remember. He thought highly of it, and advised me to get one like it. What he says about the queer hotel is all true. I don't remember that I had a headache, but we were both hungry. J.H. was very amused about something at the hotel, and we had a hearty laugh. It was connected with dirt." [7]

At the end of this and other investigations of Mrs. Piper's mediumship, philosopher William James wrote an account of his studies of the medium in 1886:

My own conviction is not evidence, but it seems fitting to record it. I am persuaded of the medium's (Mrs. Piper) honesty, and of the genuineness of her trance; and although at first disposed to think that the "hits"" she made were either lucky coincidences, or the result of knowledge on her part as to who the sitter was and of his family affairs, I now believe her to be in the possession of a power yet to be explained. [8]

Although the events described here are not exactly earthshaking, it is a good example because no one in the séance room knew anything about the events described with such feeling by the medium, Mrs. Piper. This *sounds* like full-bandwidth communication with the dead. The SPR members were aware, however, that someone living could have been the telepathic source of the information.

Among the strongest of Mrs. Piper's cases is that of George Pellew, a young philosopher who died shortly after a single anonymous visit to the medium. Although Mrs. Piper didn't know the living Pellew at all, he reappeared to her five years after his death in New York City as a "control" — an apparently independent entity or spirit guide who speaks through an entranced medium. Some researchers believe that controls are not actually external spirits, but are, rather, secondary aspects of the medium's own personality.

According to Alan Gauld, in his 1983 book *Mediumship and Survival,* Pellew, speaking through Mrs. Piper, was confronted with 150 different anonymous sitters over a period of many weeks, and was successful in identifying 29 of the 30 people who had been acquainted with Pellew when he was alive.[9] Pellew was confused by the thirtieth person, who had been a childhood friend and had changed considerably since Pellew had last seen him. Pellew carried on conversations with each of these people, dealing with intimate matters of their lives and past relationships.

Most important, *Mrs. Piper did not know the living George Pellew,* and therefore would have no way, psychically or otherwise, to identify his friends and the details of their past relationships. Mrs. Piper's dramatization of Pellew's character and his idiosyncratic modes of expression seemed so authentic that his thirty friends were convinced they had spoken with him. Each was willing to testify that they had indeed communicated with a disembodied surviving intelligence who appeared to be George Pellew. What more could poor Myers do to prove the survival of the human spirit?

Well, it appears that he was able to autonomously organize and conduct an entire double-blind experiment after his own death! These famous "cross-correspondence" experiments took place in the early 1900s between England, India, and the United States. Cross correspondence is said to occur when what is written or said by one medium, or communicator, significantly corresponds with the writings of another unrelated medium in a distant place.

This complex cross-correspondence study spanned more than

thirty years, involving five mediums on three continents. More than fifty scholarly papers have been written about this adventure, many of them book-length documents in the SPR archives. However unlikely, it appears that the posthumous Myers was continuing his demonstrations that survival of the personality was real and not just ESP by the medium.

The simplified version of the case we present here involves three highly respected mediums of the day: Mrs. M. deG. Verrall, a classics lecturer at Cambridge and the wife of A.W. Verrall, a well-known classics scholar; Mrs. Fleming, a resident of India and the sister of author Rudyard Kipling; and Mrs. Piper in the United States. For twenty years after his death in 1901, messages from the deceased Myers appeared in the entranced writings of these widely separated mediums, and several others. The messages were fragmentary and full of partial references to very obscure Greek and Latin poetry. The poetry had been well-known to Myers, but unknown to the others, except Mrs. Verrall, who had had slight contact with it many years previously.

The information that found its way to the SPR in London was examined by five indefatigable researchers, including the famous physicist Sir Oliver Lodge. Brian Inglis describes "this elaborate code designed to prove the reality of spirit communication" in his book *Natural and Supernatural:* "To each automatist the information would be so fragmentary and strange as to be meaningless; but when pieced together, it could carry information of a kind that only could have come from Myers. . . . " [10]

Runki's Leg

This next case from the 1930s is remarkable as much for the passion exhibited by the deceased communicator as for the information he provided. It is a complex case involving a communicator who pleaded with the participants sitting with a medium in Iceland to help him find his missing leg! The circle had been meeting from time to time in 1937 and 1938 when an uncouth spirit named Runolfur Runolfsson, or "Runki," appeared. Runki was completely unknown to anyone in the circle.

The case, known as "Runki's Leg," is significant for several reasons: The material that appeared could not have been clairvoyantly perceived by the medium from any single document or obituary, nor telepathically obtained from a single living person. Even though these events occurred in Reykjavik in the 1930s, they were investigated by two of the world's most experienced and knowledgeable psychic researchers, American Dr. Ian Stevenson and Dr. Erlander Haraldsson from Iceland. Author Alan Gauld writes in *Mediumship and Survival* that Runki "showed a yearning for snuff, coffee, and alcohol, refused to give his name, and kept reiterating that he was looking for his leg. Asked where his leg was, he replied that it was 'in the sea.' " [11]

In 1939 a new sitter named Ludvik joined the circle and became the focus of questions from the communicator Runki, speaking through the medium. Runki revealed that he had been drinking with friends in October of 1887 — over fifty years earlier. On his way home that night, Runki said that he lay down and fell asleep on the rocky seashore, was swept out to sea, and drowned: "I was carried in by the tide, but the dogs and ravens tore me to pieces." He told the sitters that the remnants of his body were buried in a nearby graveyard, but his thighbone was missing. The bone "was carried out again to sea, but was later washed up at Sandgerti. There it was passed round, and now it is in Ludvik's house."

Ludvik knew nothing about the bone. But inquiries among the oldest people in the community turned up memories of a very tall man's leg bone that had been found on the beach. For reasons that no one could remember, the bone had been put into the interior wall of the house now occupied by Ludvik. The bone was then retrieved from inside the wall of Ludvik's house, and it was verified that Runki had indeed been a very tall man.

Most astonishing is the passionate purpose of the communicator. No mere phantom appearing at the foot of your bed, he appeared to a specific sitter with a purpose. One of many interesting questions, however, remains unanswered: Why was the spirit of Runki still looking for his leg fifty years after his death? We could conjecture that he was caught in some transition because of his intense interest in his previous body.

In the following discussion, we show that the great religions philosophies suggest that spirits may actually find new bodies for themselves.

Reincarnation and the Perennial Philosophy

F.W.H. Myers devoted a good part of his life, and perhaps several of his posthumous years as well, to the question of whether some aspect of ourselves will live again. The data and research from the SPR offer considerable evidence that identifiable memories from a previous life survive the death of the body. In our present lives, by quieting our minds we can have the direct experience that so moved Tolstoy: the feeling of unity with the infinite. But this does not, obviously, demonstrate that we have an opportunity to live again. While good data exists that some aspect of our previous self survives, we don't recommend that you postpone projects for the "next lifetime."

The question of surviving awareness relates directly to the question of our nonlocal connection to the infinite, and the concept that time can be transcended. Since the Hindu and Buddhist mystics so accurately described nonlocal mind, we might also take comfort from their core teaching on the subject of surviving awareness. The Bhagavad Gita, recorded in the first or second century AD, addresses the issue directly: "As during our lifetime we survive the death of the baby body, the young body, and the mature body successively and retain our individuality, so after the death of the old body we shall survive, live, and retain our individuality, and continue to exist throughout eternity." [12]

The Buddhist teachings agree with the Hindu. Although the Buddha was thought to have lived about five hundred years before Christ, several centuries before the Gita appeared, the ideas in both teachings are so similar it almost seems that he read a prepublication copy of the Bhagavad Gita. Indeed the ideas all come from the ancient Indian teachings known as the Vedas, which predate both the Buddha and the Bhagavad Gita by hundreds of years.

The following verses appear in a long and beautiful poem that Buddha recited to his close friends. They summarize many of his essential teachings on both reincarnation and suffering:

> I, Buddha, who wept with all my brother's tears,
>> Whose heart was broken by a whole world's woe
> Laugh and am glad for there is liberty!
>> Know you who suffer! know you suffer from yourselves.
>
> The Books say well each one's life
>> The outcome of his former living is.
> The bygone wrongs bring forth sorrows and woes
>> The bygone right brings bliss.
>
> Who toiled a slave may come next life a prince.
>> For gentle worthiness and merit won;
> Who ruled a King may wander earth in rags
>> For things done and undone. [13]

The Christian Afterlife

As we described earlier, many of the more transcendental teachings of Jesus agreed with Hindu and Buddhist beliefs of the time. We now understand from Gnostic documents unearthed in the late 1800s that these ideas were carried on by the Gnostic Christians in the first few centuries AD. For example, Jesus, speaking to his disciples, says in

John 10: 15–18, "I lay down my life for the sheep. And I have other sheep that are not of this fold. I must bring them also, and they will heed my voice. . . . For this reason the Father loves me. Because I lay down my life that I may take it up again. No one takes it from me, but I lay it down of my own accord. I have power to lay it down, and I have power to take it again." [14]

The Gnostic Christians believed in reincarnation as part of a belief system that stressed individual will and personal connection with God. Not surprisingly, the Church of Rome opposed this kind of freelance spirituality. In the *Pistis Sophia* — the collection of Gnostic Gospels discovered in the nineteenth century — Jesus and John converse at length on the subject of rebirth after death:

> John persists with still another question. "What will happen to a person who has committed no sin . . . yet has not found the mysteries?" "Such a person before birth," says Christ, "does not drink the waters of forgetfulness. He receives rather a cup filled with thoughts of wisdom and soberness in it. He is then reborn into a body which can neither sleep nor forget because of the cup of soberness that has been handed to it. It will whip his heart persistently to question about the mysteries of the Light until he finds them. . . ." [15]

The Jewish Afterlife

As with so many other things, the Jews hold all possible opinions about the afterlife. We know that the Old Testament condemns any practice that appears to come from Pagan sources and, therefore, challenges monotheism. As Simcha Rafael points out in *Jewish Views of the Afterlife,* Old Testament Deuteronomy (18:10) clearly prohibits mediumship, indicating the practice was known and ongoing: "Let no one be found among you who . . . is a medium or spiritist, or who consults the dead." [16]

In case the issue of an afterlife is still misunderstood, the finality of death is spelled out in Ecclesiastes 9:9: "Go thy way, eat thy bread with joy, and drink thy wine. Whatsoever thy hand findeth to do, do it with thy might, for there is no work, nor device nor knowledge, nor wisdom in the grave whither thou goest."

Simcha Rafael writes that if you stop a Jew on the street and ask him, "What do Jews believe about the afterlife?" he or she will say that Jews believe in an afterlife but won't be able to give any detail. "We, of course, have a soul," they might say, but beyond that it's murky. By and large Judaism celebrates life and living, dwelling on the preciousness of life here rather than in the hereafter.

While this may realistically describe Main Street Judaism today, a rich and powerful subtext has been gaining strength in recent years. An increasing number of Jews are reclaiming their connections to mystical Judaism, as reflected in the teachings of the Baal Shem Tov, Hassidic Judaism, and the Kabbalah. Almost all of this resurgence stems from worldwide interest in Jewish Renewal, or "What ever happened to Jewish spirituality?" Rafael says modern Jews with some personal experience of God fear not so much death but judgment from the other side.

To add to the confusion on this question, Rabbi Moses Maimonides, the twelfth-century sage whom many Jewish scholars consider the "wisest of the wise," forcefully argued for the survival of the soul:

> The resurrection of the dead is one of the cardinal principles established by Moses, our teacher. . . . A person who does not believe in this principle has no real religion. He certainly does not cleave to the Jewish religion.
>
> When one attains complete humanity, he acquires what is of the nature of the perfect human being, namely there is no external force which can deny his soul eternal life. [17]

Simcha Rafael tells the story of Rabbi Elimelekh of Lyzhansk, who was extraordinarily cheerful as his death approached. When a disciple asked him to explain, the Rabbi replied, "Why should I not rejoice, seeing that I am about to leave the world below, and enter into the higher worlds of eternity. Do you not recall the words of the Psalmist: 'Yea though I walk through the valley of death, I shall fear no evil, for you are with me?' Thus does the Grace of God display itself." [18]

We are writing here not about the God of our childhood, not the God with a white beard who lives in the sky and will love us if we're good and punish us if we're bad. We sympathize with the modern atheist who is unable to believe in such a God. The God the dying rabbi understood is the God of unlimited love — available to be experienced by anyone willing to chance opening their heart to such a frightening possibility.

Old Souls in New Bodies

Does any evidence encourage us to believe that we mortals may be able to *"lay it down, and take it up again?"* The answer is yes — provided to us by the monumental work of psychiatrist Ian Stevenson at the University of Virginia Medical School. Since 1960, Stevenson has been investigating cases in which children, usually three to five years old, begin relating memories of an earlier life to their parents. In his first book, *Twenty Cases Suggestive of Reincarnation,* these children often provided detailed memories of their "previous" wives, husbands, children, and houses. Frequently, they have graphic memories of how they died, and, in some cases, who killed them. [19]

In the most valuable of Stevenson's cases, the children's previous families lived in distant cities or villages, and were unknown to the children's present parents. In an important subclass of cases, these young children demonstrated surprising skills and information, such as relating memories in a language different than that spoken by their parents. In one case, a young person spoke Bengali in a family that spoke Tamil. In another, a child skillfully played a musical instrument he had never seen before. Although the majority of these children with memories and abilities from a previous life live in Asian countries where reincarnation is a common belief, Stevenson has published over eighty papers in recent years showing memories in children from European and North American families as well.

To verify these remarkable claims, both the child's family members and the distant family are interviewed, ideally before the two families meet. When the families are united, profound emotions often follow. One five-year-old boy greeted his ostensible former wife and children, showing the emotions appropriate for an adult and remarkable for a little boy. Often the child is able to name many former family members and friends. Surprisingly often, the child is able to locate money hidden in the house, frequently to the embarrassment of a surviving family member.

These previous life memories are not necessarily evidence of reincarnation. Rather, they present additional data for the idea that *something* nonphysical does survive our death — be it our thoughts, memories, intentions, or emotional connections. These aspects of our nonlocal consciousness may endure in our world of space and time long after our bodies have returned to earth. We might, then, give thought to the quality of these desires, memories, thoughts, and emotions. What do we leave behind, besides our stuff? Can we consciously change these mindforms, which may outlive us?

Dr. Stevenson's most recent investigations are even more bizarre than those involving remembered memories. In these cases, children with memories of a past life also have birthmarks or physical deformities that correspond to injuries received in the remembered previous lives. In his book *Where Reincarnation and Biology Intersect,* Stevenson shows graphic photos of children and adults who have physical deformities, corresponding to medical reports and x-rays of the person whom the child remembers as a previous incarnation. [20] In all his studies, however, Stevenson has found that the children eventually forget their ostensible memories from previous lives by the time they reach the age of eight or ten. [21]

What Is Reincarnation?

Having said this much, the logical question remains about *what* could possibly be reincarnating. In one case the child says, "I am really a wealthy Brahman with a home in Bombay," yet he seems to be a clerk's son living in Calcutta. The child has verifiable memories of an earlier life that did, in fact, occur to somebody. But the experiences obviously did not occur to the body claiming the memories. The child knows he's a child, but at the feeling level he wants to drink cognac with his mistress, as he did in the old days.

Before we are overwhelmed with the idea of born-again souls, it would be wise to define reincarnation with what we observe, to separate it from all the different belief systems that lay claim to it. Philosopher Robert Almeder has minimally defined the term in a 1997 *Journal of Scientific Exploration* essay:

> There is something essential to some human personalities, . . . which we cannot possibly construe solely in terms of either brain states, . . . or biological properties caused by the brain. . . . [F]urther, after biological death, this nonreducible biological trait sometimes persists for some time, in some way, in some place, existing independently of the person's former brain and body. Moreover, after some time, some of these irreducible essential traits of human personality . . . come to reside in other human bodies, either some time during the gestation period, at birth, or shortly after birth. [22]

The Bishen Chand Case

The following of Stevenson's examples meets almost all his requirements for a perfect case suggesting reincarnation: data were collected by an outside observer as the case progressed; the families didn't meet until long after recording the substantial information; nearly all the people involved were still alive; the young child showed skills in music and foreign language; and, with memories, the child located hidden items. Robert Almeder described the case in his splendid 1992 book

Death and Personal Survival: The Evidence for Life After Death. [23]

Bishen Chand Kapoor was born in 1921 in the city of Barielly, India. At about one and a half, he began asking questions about a town called Pilibhit, some fifty miles away. No one in his family knew anyone who lived in Pilibhit. By the time Bishen Chand was five, he remembered his previous life quite clearly.

He had been named Laxmi Narain, the son of a wealthy land owner. He claimed to remember an uncle named Har Narain, who actually turned out to be the father of his remembered self. The young Bishen Chand described the house of Laxmi Narain, as well as a neighbor's house with a green gate, and how he had enjoyed the singing and dancing of the young women who entertained men in bars. He often spoke and read words of Urdu, a language written in Arabic script, even though Hindi was the language spoken in Bishen Chand's house.

A local attorney heard about Bishen Chand's memories and came to the house to record statements from the boy and other family members. In one of the most surprising memories, the boy recounted killing a suitor of his mistress, showing surprising awareness for a five year old of the difference between wife and mistress. Not quite eight years had elapsed since the death of the adult Laxmi Narain.

When the attorney, along with the young Bishen Chand and Chand's father, traveled to Pilibhit, it was immediately confirmed that a man named Laxmi Narain had indeed shot and killed a rival lover of a prostitute who was still in the town. Narain had avoided prosecution because of his wealth but had died two years later, at age thirty-two. When taken to Laxmi's old school, the boy ran to the classroom, described the teacher, and from an old photograph, identified and named classmates, one of whom was in the crowd that had gathered. Chand had a heartwarming reunion with Laxmi's mother, whom he greatly preferred to his own. The green gate was seen as described, and when given Laxmi's tabla drums, he was reported to have played them with great skill. Before leaving the house, he revealed where he had hidden a treasure of gold coins, which were recovered the next day.

This story suggests that something survives. No amount of ESP on the part of the five-year-old child could produce the skills and the range of adult emotions he displayed. In addition, the identification of unknown people by name from a photograph far exceeds anything we have seen in the annals of ESP research. To us, the data strongly suggest that these memories have a verifiable basis in actual past events.

The childhood appearance of memories, birthmarks, and deformities related to a previous life is consistent with the Eastern belief in the law of karma — the law of cause and effect, or action and reaction. Eastern spiritual philosophies also teach that these memories of past desires and attachments, called *samscara* in Sanskrit, represent a critically important opportunity for us to learn compassion and gain wisdom as we move from one lifetime to another. For example, knowing you were strangled in a past lifetime is better than having been strangled and not knowing it, especially if you suffer from a recurrent stiff neck.

So far, this survey of evidence for the survival of some aspect of our being beyond bodily death has included wisdom teachings from throughout the world, past-life memories, and after-death communications through psychic mediums, as well as dreams and spirit apparitions. Our last form of evidence is wholly contemporary, coming from a woman who in 1988 was the first recipient of a heart-lung transplant in New England. Her stranger-than-fiction account raises the question of whether the body's cells or organs carry their own memories of a person's essence, and whether such memories can move from body to body.

Chicken Nuggets Beyond the Grave?

A high school drama teacher, Claire Sylvia was the parent of a teenaged daughter who lived near Boston. She was also an accomplished dance teacher and performer before a chronic lung disease damaged her heart and left her unable to breathe properly. She was fortunate enough to receive a heart-lung transplant at Yale-New Haven hospital in 1988, from which she recovered swiftly. This first heart-lung transplant in New England generated considerable television and newspaper publicity. Reporters continued to visit her throughout her hospital stay.

On the third day after her surgery, a reporter asked, "Claire, now that you've had this miracle, what do you want more than anything else?"

Much to her surprise, she exclaimed, "A beer!" In her book, *A Change of Heart,* she describes her confusion over her response:

> I was mortified that I had answered this sincere question with such a flippant response. I was also surprised, because I didn't even like beer. At least, I never had before. But the craving I felt at that moment was specifically for the taste of beer. For some bizarre reason, I was convinced that nothing else in the world could quench my thirst.
>
> That evening, after the reporters had left, an odd notion occurred to me: maybe the donor of my new organs . . . had been a beer drinker. Was it possible, I wondered, that my new heart had reached me with its own set of tastes and preferences? [24]

The identity of organ donors in such cases is almost never revealed to the recipient, and Sylvia was denied that information by hospital officials. As her recovery progressed, she found her energy level becoming almost frenetic at times. She felt much more assertive, even aggressive. Her lung capacity, physical exuberance, and libido became more robust than ever before, even after full recovery and dancing again professionally. She began to seek out physically challenging forms of recreation, such as riding a motorcycle, or taking rigorous outdoor hikes. Her daughter and a friend chided that her formerly graceful gait had become "lumbering, like a football player." Always a confirmed heterosexual, she now began to find herself

attracted to women whom she, "as a woman, didn't feel were especially attractive" — such as short blond ones — and to have dreams
in which she was marrying a woman.

In short, Claire Sylvia began to feel that she had taken on a new
personality — the personality of a robust teenage boy — along with
her new heart and lungs. She believed she had inherited the traits of
a young man named Tim, whom she believed to be her organ donor,
and who visited her in recurring dreams. Her hunch about Tim
became an obsession when she found herself craving the taste of
green peppers and, of all things, chicken nuggets, which she had formerly found revolting.

A psychic friend who dreamed about her donor's death notice
helped her to locate her donor's obituary "in the middle of the page
of a Maine newspaper." Following the friend's intuition, they located
a death notice of a teenaged man in Maine on the day of Sylvia's
transplant operation. The discovery led to her meeting with her
donor's family. The family confirmed that Sylvia's heart and lungs
had belonged to a restlessly energetic young man, who had died in a
motorcycle crash with a bag of chicken nuggets under his jacket. He
had loved green peppers and beer, had a short blond girlfriend, and
had possessed many of the same personality characteristics that Claire
had felt mingling with her own. Over time, the parents and siblings
of her teenaged donor welcomed Claire Sylvia into their family.

Sylvia's experiences led her to organize a support group for others in her area who had transplanted organs, and she discovered that
many of them had similar sensations of inheriting another person's
mannerisms and preferences along with their donated organs. One
man who lost his sense of rhythm and skills for dancing and playing
sports believed he had received a heart from a sedentary person. A
shy, introverted, and racially prejudiced Caucasian man became talk-
ative and interested in civil rights after his transplant.

Sylvia began to interview organ transplant recipients whenever possible. Though they were reluctant to reveal perceptions they knew would provoke skepticism, she found they had experienced a variety of surprising character changes after receiving their new organs. Some of these changes included adopting a new vocabulary and modes of expression, developing a proclivity for yelling profanities despite being a born-again Christian, and replacing a phobia of water with the desire to go boating and swimming. Another found himself attracted to a particular pew in an unfamiliar church and feeling he knew the priest. All told, changes ranged from transforming from a fastidiously neat to a casually messy person, to even seeing apparitions and sensing the presence of their donor's spirit.

The most commonly noted changes were new food preferences, especially among people with kidney transplants. For instance, one steak-lover became a vegetarian, and a man who had never liked coffee received a kidney from his coffee-craving sister and soon became a coffee lover, too.

In some cases, the recipients felt that these acquired personality changes gradually dissipated over time. For others, the regression back to their former selves was more rapid. Many of the transplant recipients sensed that their donor's spirit or memories eventually moved on.

The unusual stories in *A Change of Heart* raise questions similar to others discussed in this chapter. Does some aspect of our self endure after our body dies? Do we have a spirit that, for a time after our death, may affect or communicate with the living? Could it be that when people die suddenly and unexpectedly, such as occurs in murders or accidents, their spirits become caught between the two dimensions of life and the hereafter, and attach themselves to another person, causing other people, including psychic mediums, to inherit or access their memories and preferences?

Psychologist Carl Jung believed that spirits of the dead are created by those who die but remain psychologically attached to someone living. Such spirits, according to Jung, are activated by intense emotions or unresolved needs, presumably on the part of either the dead person or the living one, or some interaction involving their emotional connection. [25]

Others have hypothesized that the memories and emotions may be imbedded in our cells or organs, and that this information can be accessed by the brain of a transplanted organ recipient.

We believe that the transfer of memory need not depend on the cell at all, because our minds are nonlocal — not located inside our brains or bodies. According to Rupert Sheldrake, "our minds are more like television sets than video recorders; a television tunes in to transmissions, but it doesn't store them." [26] We agree with author Dr. Larry Dossey's idea that some aspect of the donor's consciousness is fundamentally united with the consciousness of the recipient, and that receiving the donor's heart somehow intensified an already-present mental connection.

The important thread running through all these examples is that awareness persists, and that our minds are powerful. Our memories and our present thoughts affect the thoughts and experiences of ourselves and others in the future. Our memories, emotions, and intentions create information that can be accessed in nonordinary states of awareness, such as mediumistic trances, and dreams.

We can influence which information we are able to access from the greater nonlocal mind by training our minds in methods that differ from rational thought or analysis. So much of our functioning capacity as humans is frittered away in fretting over the future, regretting the past, judging others and chastising ourselves in the present, and dwelling on resentments. We often feel depressed, fearful, or anxious — all simply created by reacting to our own random thoughts and mental debris. All the world's spiritual philosophies teach a more rewarding way to live this life we are given. It involves managing our undisciplined minds.

Of all the approaches to survival discussed thus far, we are probably most comfortable with the succinctly expressed views of the Indian sage Ramana Maharshi:

> The real Self is continuous and unaffected. The reincarnating ego belongs to the lower plane, namely thought. . . . On whatever plane the mind happens to act, it creates a body for itself; in the physical world, a physical body; and in the dream world a dream body. . . .
>
> It should now be clear that there is neither real birth, nor real death. It is the mind which creates and maintains the illusion of reality in this process, till it is destroyed by Self-realisation. [27]

The cases described in this chapter, taken together with the experiments described in the previous chapter, offer strong evidence that we each stand at the center of a vast personal coordinate system, in which we can see in all directions and remember both the past and the future. As we learn to participate in this expanded awareness of space and time, past and future, we create the opportunity to experience the transcendence described by the world's mystics.

The Perennial Philosophy declares that expanded awareness can be consciously cultivated. In a quiet and safe place, we can become aware of our essential, timeless nature — that omnipresent part of ourselves, interwoven in a spiritual web connected to all.

In the previous chapter, we discussed the evidence contemporary science presents for our mind-to-mind connections. We also addressed a number of reasons why a person might want to explore learning to mind his or her own mind, and become aware of these connections. In the next chapter, we explore the evidence for our ability to *create peace in our own minds, as well as to enhance the well-being of others.* We are powerful cocreators in a participatory universe, and we can each positively affect this world, every second, even from an armchair.

CHAPTER
5

Using Our Mind to Change Our Life

The Healing Effects of the Mind —
On Ourselves and Others

Most people live, whether physically, intellectually or morally, in a very restricted circle of their potential being. They make use of a very small portion of their possible consciousness.
— William James

Most of the time it seems that we each have our own separate mind, encased within our own separate brain. But an increasing amount of research is confirming our experience that mind is unbounded by individual brains, bodies, time, or space. In the previous chapter we described experiences and experiments that demonstrate the nonlocal nature of consciousness. We provided examples of people accessing information from memories, emotions, desires, and intentions through altered states of awareness. In this chapter we explore the idea that we are each infused with consciousness, or spirit, that animates and activates both our minds *and* our bodies.

Our individual minds are embedded in a much larger nonlocal awareness, which gives each of us the potential to act as a cocreator in our world. We are much more than the impotent effects of random causes; we each possess the potential to affect the course of our lives and the lives of others. It is time for us to recognize our potential, and to learn to use it for the good of ourselves and our loved ones.

The field of psychoneuroimmunology and the healing effects of imagery, affirmations, meditation, psychotherapy, and biofeedback are all well explained in other writings, so we will only briefly address how the management of our minds and the focusing of our attention can relax and improve the health of our *own* bodies. Our focus here, however, is the landmark research illustrating how one person's concentrated attention can affect healing of *another person*. Our purpose is to explore the body of scientific research that shows that our minds are truly nonlocal, and to lay the foundation to explore, in later chapters, the power of prayer.

Experience with Healing

Although this body of scientific evidence is substantial, we wouldn't feel the passionate necessity to share these ideas if our personal experience had not shown us the truth of nonlocal mind. One of us (Jane) has practiced as a spiritual healer for more than twenty years, after being taught, or given, this ability in a near-death-like dream she experienced after praying for relief from intractable pain. Spiritual healers regularly immerse themselves in a nonordinary state of awareness that affects the psychological and physical state of their patients. Jane describes a recent spiritual healing event in which she experienced a vibrant current of loving energy radiating through her and affecting the people congregated around her in a church sanctuary:

No one expected anything out of the ordinary. I expected to give a short talk to the congregation on spiritual emergence experiences and how spiritual healing relates to our nonlocal nature. Because the church was being renovated at the time, a huge awning served as its sanctuary. The minister, Reverend Marge Britt of Unity Church in Tustin, California, asked if I would give a short demonstration of healing in the front of the church to any willing congregants. I agreed, expecting to perform an abbreviated version of my procedure, which I usually do in a private place, with one patient at a time.

People began to line up in the side aisle, and as they approached me one by one, I had a short healing interaction with each of them. To heal, I open my entire being to become a clear channel for the experience I know as God, with the intention to be used for healing. To do this, I enter a state of awareness that is free of the mental barriers of self-consciousness. While in a healing interaction, I feel surges of vibrations moving through me and radiating outward. I conceive of this energy as an active, intelligent presence of love, which somehow boosts a patient's own self-healing capability. Patients usually experience these radiations as sublimely calming and often exhilarating. Many patients undergo a physical release of tension, as well as an influx of energy that dissolves pain and facilitates healing. These sensations are accompanied by heat and tingling vibrations, which one woman described as "knitting and weaving" inside her body.

As soft organ music filled the sanctuary, the minister and other church members surrounded me with their prayerful healing intentions. As people entered this peaceful cocoon of cohered minds, many were overcome with tears and feelings of nonspecific love. After four hours of merging my consciousness with more than one hundred people, the entire church seemed filled with a resonating presence of spiritual energy drawing people in. Even those initially disinterested or even repelled by the idea of approaching a spiritual healer became interested enough to recognize the afternoon as a unique and profoundly moving experience. In this extraordinary four hours, the congregation lost their separateness, and also lost their pain.

No one anticipated this event. Many noted the unusual wind swirling through the tent during the healing service. As a scientist, I would naturally have difficulty believing this kind of experience, or understanding why people would participate in such irrational behavior, if I weren't overcome by the experience of it myself. I am forever grateful to the members of all the congregations who have been open and trusting enough to allow this mystery to occur through our interactive consciousness.

In our book *Miracles of Mind,* I describe at length my experiences as a healer, and some of the remarkable healings of illness and injury that people have experienced with my help. I often have trouble believing what occurs when I become willing to serve as a channel for healing. When I asked the active presence I conceive of as God, "Why on Earth are you using *me* for *this?"* my answer was the same that Helen Schucman received when she asked why she should be chosen to write *A Course In Miracles:* "Because you'll do it!" And it's true. Spiritual healing is not about me; it occurs naturally "in spite of myself."

I *do* nothing; I simply allow an active, intelligent, organizing energy, to use me. I surrender my *self*-consciousness — the idea that I am an isolated body, separate from others. In previous years, my curiosity about what would happen overcame my reluctance to be judged a fool. Today, the spirit that animates me overtakes my mental barriers of doubt. I am filled with gratitude for being used as an instrument of help and healing in a process I do not understand. When I direct my attention within, to the source of my attention, I experience that my consciousness is not limited to my body. Infinite unbounded consciousness is present. We are all spiritual healers connected in consciousness, waiting to recognize ourselves.

Expectations and Beliefs

In his book *Flow,* University of Chicago psychologist Mihaly Csikszentmihaly writes about optimal human experience. He tells us that the struggle for establishing control over our attention is actually a battle for the self. "The control of consciousness determines the quality of life," he writes. [1]

Csikszentmihaly teaches that *our intentions are the force that keeps information in consciousness ordered.* Each person allocates his or her limited attention either by focusing it intentionally like a beam of energy, or by diffusing it in desultory, random movements. This idea parallels a basic premise of the Vedas that Patanjali taught twenty-three centuries ago: Our experiences shape themselves according to our expectations and beliefs — often reactions to the past — combined with the direction of our attention in the present.

So today's most advanced psychology agrees with the oldest recorded Asian teachings on the relationship of mind to experience. They both state that the shape and content of our lives depend on how we use our attention. "Because attention determines what will or will not appear in consciousness," Csikszentmihaly writes, "and because it is also required to make any other mental events — such as remembering, thinking, feeling, and making decisions — happen there, it is useful to think of attention as psychic energy. . . . " [2]

According to Csikszentmihaly, we *create* ourselves by how we invest this psychic energy. Our attention is energy under our control; we are free to do with it as we please. "Hence, attention is our most important tool in the task of improving the quality of our experience," he writes. We may not be able to change events, but our experience of those events is under our control. And the untapped potential of the human mind to further creativity, peace, joy, love, wisdom, and health in our life must be *intentionally cultivated.* Additionally, the powerful step of learning to control our attention to realize our spiritual potential, and transform our consciousness, *must be self-initiated.*

Mindfulness Transforms Our Bodies and Minds

We've skillfully learned to harness mechanical, chemical, and electrical power to enhance our communication and connectedness — extending our ability to transcend distance and time. Our cars, telephones, televisions, radios, home computers, and fax machines all attest to this. Yet, Jon Kabat-Zinn, author of *Full Catastrophe Living,* believes that the transformative effects on society of large numbers of people purposefully cultivating a more mindful life are potentially more powerful than all our technological advances put together.

At the Stress Reduction Clinic at the University of Massachusetts

Medical Center, which Kabat-Zinn founded in 1979, over ten thousand people have learned to empower themselves with what they already have. They learn to manage chronic medical problems, disease, and pain by taking control of their own mind. More than twenty-five other hospitals and medical centers, as well as a variety of schools and prisons around the country, also teach Kabat-Zinn's methods for reducing stress by exercising choice in how to focus one's attention.

"Mindfulness meditation" is a method of disciplining the mind by focusing on a specific thought, or by completely letting go of all thoughts and emotions and simply watching whatever arises in one's consciousness. People practicing this method report a greater sense of self-mastery, well-being, and peace. Addictive behaviors, impulsive anger, hostility, and violent tendencies are also reduced when people develop what Kabat-Zinn describes as "a deep familiarity and intimacy with the activity and reactivity of one's own mind, and some competency in navigating through one's thoughts and emotions with equanimity, clarity, and commitment." 3

The therapeutic effects on one's own health from learning to mind one's own mind are now well documented. Dr. Herbert Benson's research at Harvard Medical School has shown that people practicing his Relaxation Response are able to significantly lower their heart rate and blood pressure. This meditative practice simply entails sitting comfortably with eyes closed in a quiet place, for as little as ten minutes a session. Even sitting on the floor of a broom closet during a coffee break works. While quietly secluded, the goal is to keep ones attention focused on one word or mental image, gently bringing your attention back to the chosen focal point when distracting thoughts intrude. Maintaining an attitude of "going with the flow" is important, so distracting thoughts are simply noticed, and let go, as you guide your attention back to your designated word or image.

Benson and his associates at the Mind/Body Medical Institute in Massachusetts have measured significant decreases in the chronic pain, insomnia, PMS symptoms, cardiac arrhythmia, nausea associated with chemotherapy, depression, pain accompanying x-ray procedures, post-operative pain and anxiety, and the frequency and severity of migraine headaches in people who regularly perform such contemplative practices. [4]

No one clearly understands how one's intentions result in the contractions of one's muscles. It remains a mystery how the invisible mind moves the physical body. But we *do* know that it is more powerful than we previously thought. Twentieth century science has now documented that our thoughts affect others — that we are all interconnected through our consciousness. We aren't even alone in experiencing the effects of our own thoughts!

We are actually already hooked up to a psychic Internet — Jung's "collective unconscious." But the users are primarily those who have learned to stop their thoughts and focus their attention. They are tuning in to access and affect the exchange of information.

How do we know that our thoughts affect others? A significant body of research now exists demonstrating that one person's focused intentions can influence the biological processes of someone far away. We do not yet understand how this occurs, but the results are indisputable, and have obvious implications for our ability to facilitate healing in others. "Do unto others as you would have them do unto you" takes on new meaning when you realize we are truly all connected, as the following research studies show.

Distant Healing with AIDS Patients

An important study by Fred Sicher, Dr. Elisabeth Targ, and others has recently been published in the December 1998 issue of the *Western Journal of Medicine*. It describes the positive therapeutic effects of distant healing on men with advanced AIDS, in research carried out at the California Pacific Medical Center. [5]

The researchers defined distant healing as an act of "mentation intended to benefit another person's physical and/or emotional well-being at a distance," adding that, "It has been found in some form in nearly every culture since prehistoric time." Their research hypothesized that an intensive ten-week distant healing intervention by experienced healers located throughout the United States would benefit the medical outcomes of a population of advanced AIDS patients in the San Francisco area.

In a pilot study, twenty men with AIDS were categorized by the number of AIDS-defining illnesses they had. An equal number of men from each category were randomly assigned to either the experimental or control group. In a follow-up study of forty subjects, the men and women were carefully matched into pairs by age, T-cell count, and number of AIDS-defining illnesses. Each pair was randomly split between the group to receive distant healing, or the control group. The participants' conditions were assessed by psychometric testing and blood testing at enrollment, after the distant healing intervention, and six months later. The physicians who reviewed their medical charts did not know to which group the patients belonged.

Forty distant healers from all parts of the country took part in the study. Each of them had more than five years experience in their particular form of healing. They were from Christian, Jewish, Buddhist, Native American, and shamanic traditions, as well as secular "bio-energetic" schools of healing. Each AIDS patient in the group receiving healing was treated by a total of ten different healers on a rotating healing schedule. Healers were asked to work on their assigned patient for approximately one hour per day for six consecutive days, with instructions to "direct an intention of health and well-being" to the subject they were attending. None of the subjects in the studies ever met the healers, nor did they or the experimenters know which group anyone had been randomized into.

In the smaller pilot study, four of the ten control subjects died, while all of subjects in the treatment group survived. However, this remarkable result was possibly confounded by unequal age distributions in the two groups. In the follow-up study, age was included in the stratification.

All subjects in the follow-up study were treated with "Triple-Drug Therapy," the well-known cocktail treatment, and no deaths occurred in either the treatment or control group. Midway through the study, neither group had a significant majority of individuals who were able to correctly guess whether they were in the group receiving healing. By the end of the experiment, however, the men in the healing group were able to identify themselves with significant odds against chance, because they had many fewer opportunistic illnesses.

The treatment group experienced significantly better medical outcomes, as well as better quality-of-life outcomes, with odds of 100 to 1 on many quantitative measures. These indicators included fewer outpatient doctor visits (185 vs. 260), fewer days of hospitalization (10 vs. 68), less severe illnesses acquired during the study as measured by illness severity scores (16 vs. 43), and significantly less emotional distress.

The editor of the journal introduced the paper by writing, "The paper published below is meant to advance science and debate. It has been reviewed, revised, and re-reviewed by nationally known experts in biostatistics, and complementary medicine. . . . We have chosen to publish this provocative paper to stimulate other studies of distant healing, and other complementary practices and agents. It is time for more light, less dark, less heat."

Healing Prayer with Cardiac Patients

Considerable evidence is mounting for the healing efficacy of prayer. An earlier successful pioneering study of distant healing with hospital patients in San Francisco was reported in the mainstream *Southern Medical Journal.*[6] In 1983, physician Randolph Byrd carried out a simple experiment at San Francisco General Hospital to test the concept of healing prayer. Over a ten-month period, he studied the effects of intercessory prayer with a Catholic prayer circle on 393 male patients hospitalized with heart disease. This study was also "double-blind," in that neither the attending doctors, the researchers, nor the participating patients knew which men were receiving the experimental prayers, and which men were in the control group, until after each patient's outcome was assessed at the end of the study. Byrd's landmark healing experiment study showed that patients who received prayer experienced significantly fewer medical complications, required many fewer antibiotics and diuretics, and needed less mechanical breathing assistance than patients who received no intercessory prayer.

Distant Mental Influence of Living Systems

We take for granted the calming effects that a mother's gentle cooing has on her distressed infant, not really thinking about the effects of her soothing *intentions.*

More than thirty years of investigations show clearly that one person's focused mental attention can affect both the physiological and the mental functioning of people located at a distant place. Without a doubt, Dr. William Braud, currently the director of research at the Institute of Transpersonal Psychology in Palo Alto, California, conceived and conducted the most comprehensive investigation of distant mental influence by humans on a variety of living organisms. The distantly influenced systems he investigated over a fifteen-year period included changes in another person's electrodermal activity (galvanic skin response), blood pressure, unconscious muscular activity, and problem-solving abilities. He also conducted experiments to affect the movement of fish and small animals.

These simple experiments carried out in the laboratory demonstrate the nonlocal effects of our mind, and serve as models for the healing experiments done with patients in hospitals. Braud's research has already shown that people who are the most stressed or in most need of help in completing a mental task seem to derive the most benefit from people sending their helping intentions. [7]

Healing Red Blood Cells

Although most of Braud's highly successful work has involved increasing and decreasing the degree of relaxation of people at a distant location, we find most interesting his experiments aimed at psychically rescuing threatened red blood cells. In these experiments, participants were asked to influence the behavior of these cells, which are not normally considered to have any consciousness at all.

The blood cells were placed in test tubes of distilled water, a toxic environment for them. If the salt content of the test tube solution deviates too much from that of the blood plasma, the cell wall weakens and the cell's contents spill into the solution. Thirty-two people served as influencers in this study, and twenty tubes of blood were compared for each subject. The participants were situated in a distant room, with the task of trying to save the red blood cells in ten target tubes from destruction. The corpuscles in the ten control tubes had to fend for themselves. Braud found that the remote healers were able to significantly retard the rate of hemolysis, or bursting, in the cells of the target tubes. [8]

Most important, these experiments show that one person's mind can have effects on a living system that can't be attributed to the placebo effect or compassionate bedside manner. Also striking is the fact that those who produced the most statistically significant results were more successful in helping their own blood cells survive than cells that came from another person.

It may be that if psychic functioning is viewed as a kind of resonance, it is easier for a person to resonate with a part of themselves than with a part of another person. Healers' abilities to easily resonate with others may partially explain their power to heal others. It is important to remember that while there is no substitute for natural talent, whatever one human being is able to do is within the capacity of others as well, though it may take more learning and practice.

Olga Worrall Heals Ailing Bacteria

In the 1980s, the renowned American healer Olga Worrall took part in an experiment conducted at the University of California at Berkeley in which she was able to prolong the life of bacteria that were challenged by antibiotics. [9] Mrs. Worrall refused to consciously harm any living thing, but she was willing to attempt to heal *E. coli* bacteria that had been poisoned with tetracycline. Researchers Dr. Elizabeth Rauscher, a physicist, and biologist Dr. Beverly Rubik, showed in well-controlled, side-by-side comparison tests Mrs. Worrall's ability to extend the lifetime of the *E. coli* cells toward which she was directing her healing intentions. After four hours of exposure to the antibiotic, all of the control bacteria were dead, while a significant number of bacteria for whom she had been praying lived on.

One important finding from this study was that the healer was not able to increase the reproduction rate of the healthy bacteria colony. Rather, she was able to aid the bacteria in need of healing. This experiment was similar to the threatened red blood cells immersed in a toxic solution. The bacteria are more complex systems than red blood cells, and have the ability to reproduce. But both one-celled systems are alive, so we can therefore imagine their consciousness being intertwined with human consciousness. Experiments with cells and bacteria, as well as animals, are important in the study of distant healing because of their freedom from the human expectations that can easily lead to the placebo effect.

Waking Anesthetized Mice

In the early 1970s, Anita and Graham Watkins at the Foundation for Research on the Nature of Man in Durham, North Carolina, conducted healing studies with mice. They investigated whether experienced healers and ESP research subjects could help mice who had been anesthetized with ether wake up faster than simultaneously anesthetized control mice. In some of the experiments, the participants sat in the same room as the mice they were trying to revive; in another study, the people attempting to revive the mice were in an adjoining room, viewing the mice through a one-way mirror.

While observing the mice through a one-way mirror, the experimenter would randomly select an individual mouse for each of the thirteen healers to awaken, and choose another mouse as a control. The results of these studies were highly significant: the experimental mice averaged 25.36 seconds to revive, while the control mice averaged 30.43 seconds — 20 percent longer. The probability that this result was due to chance is less than one in one million. In all, thirty-two series were run with twenty-four trials in each series. The researchers' paper, "Possible PK Influences on the Resuscitation of Anesthetized Mice," showed that healing intent does appear to have the power to revive unconscious animals.[10] It also showed that participants who felt they had healing ability and those who scored well on previous ESP tests did far better at waking the mice than did the three members of the laboratory staff who felt they had no special healing talent.

A decade later, a similar experiment at the same laboratory was carried out by researcher Marilyn Schlitz and laboratory director Dr. Ramakrishna Rao. This experiment showed the same result, with the selected mice waking up significantly more quickly than the control mice. And again, Schlitz, a highly successful remote viewer with extensive involvement in many successful ESP experiments, was much more successful at reviving the mice than was lab director Rao.[11]

Influencing Others Via Their Video Image

At the U.S. government–funded laboratory at Science Applications International Corporation in Menlo Park, California, Schlitz and Stephen Laberge from Stanford University expanded upon Dr. William Braud's experiments involving distant mental interactions. In 1993 they measured the extent to which people unconsciously sense the telepathic influence of a distant person who is looking at their video image. Their data show that if a person simply attended fully to a distant person whose physiological activity was being monitored, he or she could influence that person's galvanic skin responses.

In their research, one person stared intently at a closed-circuit TV monitor image of the distant participant, and influenced the remote person's electrodermal (GSR) responses. [12] The observer was instructed to try to excite, wake, or startle the person whose video image they were watching. In earlier studies by Braud and Schlitz that were also successful, the influencer simply stared at a person's video image without attempting to directly influence the person. In several experimental series, Drs. Schlitz and LaBerge found that the galvanic skin response of the subjects changed significantly during the periods when their video image was stared at in another room. These changes were compared to the times when they were left psychically alone. [13]

What Does It All Mean?

From the dawn of history certain individuals in every culture have been recognized as possessing special healing gifts. The Pharaohs of ancient Egypt viewed healers as revered advisors, and the world's great religions were founded around Gautama Buddha, Jesus of Nazareth, and the prophet Muhammad, who were all gifted healers. The earliest Christians were primarily a healing community, following centuries of healing by the Hebrew prophets Elijah, Elisha, Isaiah, and Moses.

Medicine men and healing shamans throughout Africa, Asia, and the Americas held some of the most esteemed positions in their tribes. In contrast, the progression of Western thought has largely ignored the broad range of mind-to-mind healing that has functioned in other cultures. Only recently are we realizing the power of the mind to heal through the scientific method.

We simply don't understand the causal mechanism involved in these demonstrations — how the physiological functioning of one person can be affected by the thoughts of another person. But the results of over thirty years of study are indisputable. The reduction of pain and stress of a distant patient through the ministrations of psychic and spiritual healers may be the best evidence we have for a direct mind-to-mind connection between people.

In assessing relevant research in healing, a clear relationship appears between a healer's focused intention and physical changes in patients. A spiritual healer may facilitate a connection between an organizing and purposeful principle — a higher power or God — and the healed person. The experience Jane has of merging her consciousness with that of a sick or injured person, and allowing herself to be used as a conduit of divine consciousness, may promote an influx of information that Dr. William Braud describes as activating "the healee's self-healing capabilities in the direction of balance, and away from previously distorting or interfering influences."

Braud has written that efforts to isolate the source of nonlocal healing are misguided. He believes that "the 'bottom line' of all psi findings seems to be a lesson that such questions about who's doing the psi, what type of psi is it, etc., are not appropriate ones, and that such questions presuppose a world view that is different from the one that psi findings are presenting to us." [14] Braud emphasizes that such psychic events as distant healing are a "dynamic *process* that involves *a field of persons and events* — a field that is transspatial, transtemporal, and transpersonal." Braud's view fits Jane's experience of spiritual healing — an interactive process of consciousness and caring intentions.

Dr. Larry Dossey, a physician and author of numerous books on healing, has stated unequivocally that "After scrutinizing this body of data for almost two decades, I have come to regard it as one of the best kept secrets in medical science. I'm convinced that the distant, nonlocal effects are real and that healing happens." [15]

In the previous two chapters we discussed a variety of evidence that expanded awareness is available to everyone. We not only have access to an awareness of distant events and people but we are also empowered to interact with distant selves to whom we are already connected. We know from a century of research that the self is affected by events outside its immediate space and time. The self may seem like our little center of awareness, but the limits of how far it extends have yet to be determined.

Pioneering researcher Dr. Dean Radin, writing on the question of what happens to the self when the brain dies, says, "If there is an extended self that includes all selves, then perhaps individual personality is lost, but something else may continue. . . . The mystery of the self is more mysterious than is commonly supposed." [16]

Both Eastern and Western spiritual traditions agree that our ideas about our separate selves as physical bodies are misperceptions. Christianity teaches that our bodies are "temples of the Holy Spirit which is in you. . . ." (1 Cor. 6:19). Patanjali taught that our minds and bodies are objects, illumined and activated by the "Self," which is a term for boundless, pure awareness. And contemporary science corroborates that we are nonlocal beings of consciousness unlimited by distance or time.

The word "prayer" in the Aramaic language that Jesus used meant "to set a trap." The Aramaic word that became translated as God was *"Alaha,"* signifying "essence" or "life force." "To pray" meant something like to set a trap to catch the life force, or to direct one's attention to attune to our essence. When the Aramaic words that Jesus used were translated into Greek, and later retranslated into Latin and English, much of their original meaning was distorted. We don't claim to be linguists, but we *are* trying to demonstrate that the teachings of Patanjali, Ramana Maharshi, Jesus, and modern physics share important similarities.

Who Are We?

Who are we, really, and what are our potential capabilities? Should we believe the Indian sage Patanjali, who taught that with diligent practice of meditation, or the stabilization of one's focused attention, comes expanded awareness? He taught that a cultivated mind can know the past and the future; understand the sounds made by all creatures; read what others are thinking; perceive the small, distant, and concealed; understand the interior of the body; achieve perfection of the body; and a variety of other astounding abilities.

Of course, Patanjali understood that psychic abilities (called *siddhis* in Sanskrit) were also potential stumbling blocks on the path to enlightenment, or even to a momentary direct experience of our true nature. His Holiness the Dalai Lama describes enlightenment as "no separate existence." The experience of our true nature is known in Sanskrit as *sat-chit-ananda,* translated as being-consciousness-bliss/love. Patanjali explained that the quiet mind would encounter the *siddhis,* but that extrasensory perceptions would only strengthen the ego's tendency toward separateness, self-aggrandizement, and craving for power, thereby increasing our pain. It is only by quieting *all* ego-generated mind-chatter, including psychic perceptions and brilliant thoughts, that we are able to direct our attention inward to experience our unbounded awareness.

The pure force of realizing one's true nature by becoming still is said by spiritual masters to be far more powerful than all of the other *siddhis.* The masters tell us that the force of the realization is experienced as *being* unity consciousness; being an extension of it. This is what the great spiritual healer Joel Goldsmith meant when he said, "Contact with God permits spiritual power to flow into human activity." [17] We are always in contact with spiritual power, but the actual experience of it evokes its ever-present potential.

In speaking of this primary consciousness, *A Course in Miracles* tells us, "Your task is not to seek for love, but merely to seek and find all the barriers within yourself that you have built against it." And that: "It is the function of love to unite all things unto itself and to hold all things together by extending its wholeness." [18]

Spiritual healing is about the extension of wholeness, both within and among our seemingly separate selves. What is overwhelmingly clear from the data presented in this chapter is that, independent of our beliefs, we should gratefully accept any prayers offered to us — especially if we are challenged by illness.

Why Scientists Pray
Experiencing Oneness through the Quiet Mind

Prayer is a state of receptivity in which
Truth is realized without conscious thought.
— Joel Goldsmith
Spiritual Interpretation of Scripture

Thanksgiving is one day of the year when many people unaccus-
tomed to prayer express gratitude for their good fortune. We
don't necessarily associate this gratitude with a belief in God. Rather,
we simply acknowledge that our peaceful and healthy lives are not
entirely due to our own skill and wisdom, that powers and circumstances beyond our control are at least partially responsible.

Some also remember prayers of supplication from childhood,
when we pleaded for help, for good grades, for a guy or girl to notice
us. Later, we were moved by our love for others to pray for their
health with prayers of intercession. Many religions teach prayers of
appreciation for the experience of God, or the unearned help or grace
that appears in our lives. Of course, many people feel unable to relate
to such prayers because they do not believe in a God, or they don't
perceive God's active presence in their lives.

This chapter is not about these kinds of prayer. We're examining
a different kind of attention: the opportunity to experience oneness,

transcendence, or direct contact with infinite consciousness. We're examining how our culture has treated this opportunity, how different forms of this attention have developed, and how one form, Father Thomas Keating's Centering Prayer, has successfully healed people's psychological wounds. Centering Prayer leads to an experience or 'felt' presence of God. This form of attention is neither a relaxation exercise nor self-hypnosis or ESP. It is, rather, the act of lifting our everyday awareness out of confining thoughts of ourselves as separate people in separate bodies. This type of prayer leads to a state of awareness that transcends the ordinary limits of space and time.

Transpersonal Experiences

Such states of awareness, when our perceptions and capacities for understanding expand beyond the limits of our separate selves, are known as "transpersonal experiences." In these experiences one's sense of identity or self extends beyond the individual to encompass the wider cosmos. Some people describe such experiences as "consciousness expanding," and many perceive them as being intensely spiritual, even sacred. In these expanded states of awareness people directly experience their connection to life itself — to infinite being and the source of all that is.

Other people understand transpersonal experiences as "peak experiences" achievable by the psychologically well developed. Psychologists Roger Walsh and Frances Vaughan characterize these peak life events as, "brief but extremely intense, blissful, meaningful, and beneficial experiences of expanded identity and union with the universe." [1] In their classic book *Paths Beyond Ego*, Walsh and Vaughan describe the transpersonal view of humanity. Much of this chapter was influenced by the pioneering work of these two inspiring researchers, who have collected writings that show how cultures throughout history have recognized similar transpersonal experiences — mystical, spiritual, beneficial, and unitive experiences — and how

Western culture has been slow to realize their value. They write, " . . . various Eastern traditions describe whole families of peak experiences, and claim to have methods for inducing them at will. It soon became apparent that peak experiences have been highly valued throughout history, are the focus of several Asian disciplines, and yet seem to have been significantly underestimated — even pathologized — in the modern Western world." [2]

Western Psychology and the Transpersonal

Transpersonal experiences are sometimes called "higher states of consciousness" because, in them, we often experience unusual and heightened capacities and perceptions. This expanded awareness can allow us access to what has been called "state-specific information": knowledge learned or understood in one state of consciousness that cannot be easily remembered or comprehended in another. And, of course, not all alternative states of consciousness are desirable; some may even be harmful. The delirium, psychosis, and intoxication caused by addictive drugs and alcohol are well accepted to be pathological. Until the latter part of the twentieth century, however, Western psychologists labeled as pathological most states of consciousness other than waking and sleeping.

Most European and American scholars of the mind during the first half of the twentieth century adopted Freud's psychoanalytic perspective of psychology, wherein transpersonal experiences were dismissed as irrational and, therefore, abnormal. Yearnings for an experience of oneness with universal consciousness or God, for example, were said to indicate a mental disorder resulting from weak ego defenses, which, in turn, originated in childhood trauma.

The uses of nonordinary states of experience were very limited within the Western approach to psychology. Hypnosis was recognized as a means of bringing neurotic patients' repressed childhood memories to the attention of doctors, and psychoanalysts interpreted dreams to treat their patients' pathologies. So it was understood that these two states provided information unavailable in ordinary waking experience. But Western physicians and academics tended to deny the ability of altered states of consciousness to expand the potential of healthy people.

The goal of psychoanalysis was to strengthen the ego, to allow patients to master their basic instinctual urges and resist their unconscious compulsions. These natural urges meant sexuality and aggression, as Freud did not view altering one's consciousness to connect with God as a normal or healthy drive. To indicate how primitive and regressive the psychoanalytic community perceived mind disciplines to be, one prominent psychoanalyst wrote a paper in 1931 entitled, "Buddhist Training as an Artificial Catatonia." [3]

From the Freudian perspective, life consists of a series of unpredictable interactions that are inevitably filled with tension and conflict. The best we can do is develop a strong and well-integrated sense of individuality in order to defend ourselves in a hostile world. [4] In a book discussing the absence of spirituality in most American's lives, philosopher Jacob Needleman summarizes this severely limited view of who we are by saying, "Freudianism institutionalized the underestimation of human possibility." [5]

Unfortunately for all of us, this institutionalized pessimism has endured far into contemporary thinking. For too long, according to human potential movement leaders George Leonard and Michael Murphy, most of us have realized "just a fraction of our human potential," and have lived only a very restricted "part of the life we are given." [6] One of the messages of their book *The Life We Are Given* is that our minds, our very essences, are connected to cosmic, nonlocal consciousness. We are like sponges, filled with life consciousness, floating in a vast sea of consciousness that permeates us all. We are bits in the soup of unlimited possibilities. "We are chemists in the laboratory of the Infinite. What shall we create?" asked Ernest Holmes, founder of the Science of Mind teaching.

Most of Western psychology — from Freudian psychoanalysis, through behaviorism, humanism, and existentialism — ignores our nonlocal nature, and assumes that consciousness is produced by, and in, the physical brain. Our own individual physiological and biochemical processes are thought to produce our life energy and our personal mind. In other words, matter produces consciousness. And each person's mind, thoughts, and impressions are contained inside his or her individual body, bounded by one's lifetime, and disappearing at death. But these assumptions do not correlate with contemporary scientific data that suggest the exact opposite — that matter is activated by consciousness and acts as a conduit for it.

According to Freud, sexual and aggressive urges compel our behavior; spiritual impulses are simply regressive reactions to earlier conflicts with powerful parental figures. Building on Freud, behaviorists taught that we are only composites of our behavioral conditioning. And the existentialists believed the universe to be random and chaotic; we were to define our lonely, isolated selves by acting resolutely, and coping heroically before our meaningless lives were obliterated.

And then, in the now-famous 1960s, the "human potential movement," born of humanistic psychology and the ideas of Abraham Maslow, began to awaken us to our innate potential. The humanist pioneers taught us to fully develop our authentic, separate selves. We were to focus on "being real," and giving our attention to every aspect of our real selves: our feelings and reactions, our relationships and ways of communicating, our health and bodies, our creativity, and of course, our self-esteem. Above all, we were exhorted to "fully experience." Jimi Hendrix's rock music of the time challenged, "Are You Experienced?" And many people chose to fully experience life's possibilities by ingesting psychedelic drugs and other mind-enhancing — and mind-numbing — substances. "[F]or the first time in history," declare Walsh and Vaughan, "a significant proportion of the culture experienced altered states of consciousness."

Many members of this group considered their altered states to be preciously sacred. Their lives were changed. They came to realize, without question, that their awareness expanded beyond the limits of their bodies, and that their true essence was spirit. They understood that all humanity was connected to all of life in ways that far surpassed anything they had been taught. We are all familiar with the negative effects that drug use has had on our society. But the positive effects should also be acknowledged.

Walsh and Vaughan recognize what psychoactive drug use can offer in their discussion of paths people have taken throughout history to experience their sacred nature: "Some of these [drug experiences] were clearly painful and problematic. Yet others were transcendent states that demonstrated to an unsuspecting world the plasticity of consciousness, the broad range of its potential states, the limitations and distortions of our usual state, and the possibility of more desirable ones." 7

The rock music of the sixties extolled such plasticity of consciousness. The Beatles visited India to learn more about the nature of mind. Harvard psychologist Richard Alpert left academia to study the nature of consciousness in India and became Ram Dass, a revered teacher for many Americans hungry for spirituality. Alan Watts and Ram Dass, followed by Charles Tart, Ken Wilber, and other scholars, brought respectability to the study of mind disciplines, transpersonal psychology, and altered states of consciousness.

Recently, we had the good fortune to spend an evening with Ram Dass, who is recovering from a stroke. At this gathering of teachers and pioneers in the field of transpersonal psychology, he urged his audience to tell the truth about the role that psychoactive drugs have played in "opening a door into our hearts that led to an opening into the universe." He told us that we are "the fingers of God, and have a responsibility to teach what we have learned" about the transformational power of psychedelics, when used with wisdom and conscience, as part of a spiritual quest.

From the earliest recorded history, such drugs as *soma* in India, and *ayahuasca* (a mixture of naturally occurring harmaline and DMT) in South America have been used to aid the prepared mind to achieve expanded awareness. Mescaline from the *peyote* cactus and psilocybin mushrooms have been widely used and written about through history. Since the 1960s, the hallucinogenic drug LSD, and the empathogen MDMA, known as Ecstasy, have been used to break down ego boundaries, in even the most resistant cases, by allowing users to experience a glimpse of what mystics find by sitting peacefully on a rock. Walsh has recently written further about these "timeless" experiences:

> If there is one thing that is clear about psychedelics, it is that they can unleash an awesome variety of experiences. Some of the most powerful, as well as the most profound and transformative are also some of the most controversial: specifically transpersonal experiences in which the self sense expands beyond (trans) the personal or personality to encompass wider aspects of humankind, life, the world, and the universe. [8]

The road to knowing oneself, which was once, "Turn On, Tune In, Drop Out" (Timothy Leary), became "Be Here Now" (Ram Dass), and "Wake Up!" (Charles Tart). A variety of Hindu Yogis and Swamis, Sufi masters, Zen Buddhist Roshis, and Tibetan Buddhist Rinpoches began teaching groups of Americans their Asian methods and philosophies for knowing truth and acquiring peace of mind. It must be said, however, that most mainstream Americans showed no interest in learning to control their mind, to know their true nature, or to become one with God.

But the movement was not to be denied. Previously, Western scholars had thought that contemplative Oriental disciplines taught people to withdraw into themselves, and away from life, in order to escape unbearable societal conditions. Now, many well-adjusted people pursue these contemplative mental disciplines; they are certainly no longer considered pathologically regressive.

For thousands of years, contemplative Asian wisdom traditions such as Buddhism, Vedanta, and Yoga have described stages of transpersonal development and methods for stabilizing attention in order to access state-specific information. These spiritual philosophies show how to refine and stabilize states of awareness in which human perceptions and capacities expand far beyond what Westerners thought was possible.

Many philosophers and psychologists, as well as spiritual seekers and students of the Perennial Philosophy, now consider these mental disciplines to be psychologically evolutionary. They promote mental and physical health, expand awareness, and heighten desirable emotions such as peacefulness, equanimity, compassion, and altruism. In fact, in *Paths Beyond Ego,* Walsh and Vaughan present mounting evidence that suggests a lack of transpersonal or self-transcendent experiences may underlie much of the depression, angst, and meaninglessness that dominate the lives of many people today.

Author and physician Andrew Weil writes in *The Natural Mind* that the desire to alter consciousness periodically is an innate drive analogous to hunger or sexual desire. Philosopher and psychologist Abraham Maslow explained that becoming our most self-actualized selves requires the awareness-expanding effects of peak altered-state experiences. He went so far as to say that "without the transcendent and the transpersonal we get sick, violent, and nihilistic. . . . "[9] And as far back as 1901, Richard Bucke, physician to poet Walt Whitman and author of a remarkable early book on this subject titled *Cosmic Consciousness,* reminded his readers that all of the world's great religions and spiritual practices are based on one person's experience of an illumined state of expanded awareness — a person whom others revered because of his transcendence of self-consciousness and experience of union with the divine. Philosopher William James said the very concept of "spiritual" entails a process that "establishes the self — however briefly — in a larger power and sufficiency." 10

Bucke described this timeless state of transcendent consciousness that is available to us all in this way:

> Along with the consciousness of the cosmos there occurs an intellectual enlightenment of illumination which alone would place the individual on a new plane of existence — would make him almost a member of a new species. To this is added a state of moral exaltation, an indescribable feeling of elevation, elation, and joyousness, and a quickening of the moral sense. . . . With these come what may be called a sense of immortality, a consciousness of eternal life, not a conviction that he shall have this, but the consciousness that he has it already. 11

These peak experiences that Bucke describes are indeed elevating and transforming, but we don't have to become a member of a new species to experience them. We only need to be fully who we already are, and right now realize our potential as vehicles of transforming consciousness. Putting this realization into action is truly revolutionary, just as being happy and at peace in this world are revolutionary acts. Becoming peaceful and happy depend upon a revolution in ourselves.

These attitudes are not things some of us are born with and others are not. Buddhist teacher Sharon Salzberg writes in *Loving-Kindness,* "The difference between misery and happiness depends on what we do with our attention." 12 Since we continually create a field of influences in our lives by our *intentions,* she says it is important that we become aware of the intentions that drive our actions. Buddhism teaches that the roots of the painful conditions we experience are ignorance of how our attention creates our experience by clinging to transitory circumstances beyond our control. Being aware of how our mind behaves is key. That's why Indian sage Nisargadatta Maharaj taught that "Intelligence is the door to freedom, and alert attention is the mother of intelligence." [13]

Meditation: Alert Attention

Wisdom teachers universally teach that inner calm cannot be attained through some secret mind manipulation that magically suppresses our train of thought, or converts stressful thoughts to peaceful ones. We can't willfully stop our thoughts by shutting them out of our attention. Instead, these teachers encourage us to see our thoughts clearly, notice them come and go, and deliberately position ourselves differently in relationship to them. This process is known as mindfulness meditation, which Jon Kabat-Zinn describes in *Wherever You Go There You Are* as "Letting the mind be just as it is, and knowing something about how it is in this present moment." [14] In the words of Yogi Swami Satchitananda, a popular meditation teacher in the United States in the 1970s, "You can't stop the mind waves, but you can learn to surf!"

Vietnamese monk Thich Nhat Hanh calls meditation the art of letting one form of energy transform another, a similar concept to asking Jesus Christ to come into your life and being reborn in the spirit. Eastern wisdom teachers developed various meditation techniques for bringing the mind to a standstill, a prerequisite for this transformation of thoughts of separation to the experience of oneness.

Buddhist training involves three basic approaches that aim at expanded awareness and, eventually, enlightenment. One central technique is the art of concentrating on one single thing so that the mind enters a state of one-pointedness. The focus of attention may be an object, a part of the body, a thought, the space between thoughts, a sound, all sounds, a sacred word, or, as in Zen, a riddle or *koan*. With single-pointed attention, eventually even mental focus falls away, revealing our natural state of pure awareness.

Buddhist teacher Thich Nhat Hanh shares this simple method of bringing our attention to the single-pointed focus of appreciation for this present moment — the only time we can experience either peace or the presence of God. He suggests that we silently repeat these four phrases while noticing our breathing:

> Breathing in, I calm my body
> Breathing out, I smile.
> Dwelling in the present moment,
> I know this is a wonderful moment! [15]

Most Asian forms of meditation stress developing an awareness of one's breathing. Yoga includes many breathing exercises and techniques, whereas Buddhist practices such as Thich Nhat Hanh's stress simple awareness of the breath. A third method for stilling the mind is to concentrate on the body, usually by sitting motionless and *experiencing* the body's sensations, rather than thinking about them.

All of these techniques aim at stopping the flow of one's stream of consciousness. Single-pointed concentration leads to a falling away of all thoughts. Focusing your attention on bodily sensations allows you to realize that you are not your body, but that which is *aware* of your body. And becoming mindful of our breathing leads to an awareness of and reverence for the life within us — the spiritual core of our being.

Buddhism then teaches the importance of three elements, or jewels, of the spiritual path: a teacher (the Buddha), a body of teaching (the *dharma),* and a loving, nonviolent spiritual community (the *sangha).* Meditation without these supports can lead to a pathological loss of the self, without the desired effects of joy, peace, and love.

Spiritual practice, according to Salzberg, "uncovers the radiant, joyful heart within each of us and manifests this radiance to the world." [16] The Buddha described a spiritual path that frees us from the illusion of being separated from others as "the liberation of the heart, which is love." And Kabat-Zinn explains that "practice" in Buddhism is not meant in the usual sense of repetitive rehearsing, as there is no "performance." Practice means that we commit fully, with pure intention, to dwell in each moment in stillness.

It is time for Westerners to realize that the teachings of the Buddha are centered around kindness, compassion for all suffering, and noninjury to life — all very similar to the teachings of Jesus. The *experience* of unity consciousness and its transformative *effects* are at the core of both Christian and Buddhist traditions. The state of mind sought through Buddhist meditation is known as "the void," a term that sometimes disturbs Westerners. This void is not nothing; it is no *thing* and no *thought* — the unnamable, active, pure awareness that infuses us with energy, clear sight, and loving intentions. If we can move beyond the concept of God being a bearded man in the sky, we can understand what Thich Nhat Hanh means when he says, "When you are a truly happy Christian, you are also a Buddhist. And vice versa." [17]

"Mind Creates the Abyss, the Heart Crosses It"

The Indian saint Ramana Maharshi declared, "All scriptures without exception proclaim that for salvation, mind should be subdued." [18] And when asked why thoughts prevented a person from experiencing God, contemporary Vedanta sage Sri Nisargadatta Maharaj told his students that an individual's mind tends to consider itself isolated, and generally functions by making distinctions. It is love that allows us to know God:

> Maharaj: The mind, by its very nature, divides and opposes. Can there be some other mind, which unites and harmonizes, which sees the whole in the part and the part as totally related to the whole?
> [Q: The other mind — where to look for it?]
> Maharaj: In the going beyond the limiting, dividing, and opposing mind. In ending the mental process as we know it. When this comes to an end, that mind is born.
> [Q: In that mind, the problems of joy and sorrow exist no longer?]
> Maharaj: Not as we know them, as desirable or repugnant. *It*

becomes rather a question of love seeking expression and meeting with obstacles. The inclusive mind is love in action, battling against circumstances, initially frustrated, ultimately victorious.

[Q: Between the spirit and the body, is it love that provides the bridge?]

Maharaj: What else? Mind creates the abyss, the heart crosses it. [italics ours] [19]

"I" is a thought of separation, including separation from God. Thoughts arise from a part of infinite mind perceiving itself as separate, so thoughts impede a transcendent experience of oneness. Spiritual traditions, however, declare it is the pain of feeling separate and unwhole that draws us to seek connection with God, or realize our true selves.

The first step to mastering inner silence is to be still, and that is best done by secluding oneself. So the process of realizing unity consciousness, Sanskrit scholar Dean Brown tells us, starts with separating ourselves from other people, and separating our thoughts from material things that promote an "outgoing mind." We "go into our closet," or alone "into the desert," to realize union with God, or indwelling spirit.

Patanjali taught that an individual's intellect tended to attribute the power of consciousness to itself. He said our illusory sense of our separate selves comes from this egoistic tendency, and that thinking is unable to transcend itself to access a higher dimension of truth. According to Patanjali, our mind is another organ of the body. Like the eye, which is illumined by light but does not create it, the human mind is a perceiver of consciousness but does not create it. Rather, it is consciousness or awareness that activates and informs the contents of the mind. Because an individual's mind and thoughts are so reactive to any sensory input that happens to grab its wayward attention, thinking must be transcended for union with Divine Consciousness. The very first sentence of Patanjali's *Sutras* says: "Union *(Yoga)* is mind-wave quieting." [20]

What we *can* expect from an experience of union with God, according to Christian mystic Joel Goldsmith, is a total absence of one's usual self-consciousness: "We find within ourselves a great sense of love, a great sense of joy and freedom, a great desire just *to be.*"[21] He goes on to say that this loving energy source manifests itself in a person as a healing consciousness. When we regularly align ourselves with Infinite Consciousness, a current of healing information or energy flows through us, because loving awareness seeks to extend itself through quiet, receptive minds. So we are all potential spiritual healers.

Why Scientists Pray

All spiritual paths teach that experiences of union with the divine promote health, as well as enlighten, through a continual process of consciousness renewal and expansion. But Westerners who take up yoga as a form of gymnastics or fitness training or who meditate solely to relieve the stress of freeway driving or parenting teenagers are ignoring the ultimate goal of these practices. The spiritual processes many people use to enhance their body or their self-image are actually powerful tools for the *transcendence* of the body, and everything personal or self-conscious.

Wisdom teachers say that you can recognize a person who "knows God" and experiences such union by his or her tendency toward self-*less*-ness, or, rather, an expanded sense of self that includes an intimate connection with all life. Equanimity in difficult situations, kindness and generosity, nonjudgment toward others, and a sense of inner tranquillity and causeless joy are other indicators of spiritual awareness. Psychic powers are not the criteria to look for in a teacher. Instead, we are advised to look for love and kindness.

All religious rituals and practices have as their ultimate goal the relinquishment of self-consciousness — to relinquish our attachment to our body, thoughts, memories, imagination, concepts of time, and all the sensory stimuli that usually attract or repel our attention. When we stop constantly relating every perception we have to our self — stop comparing, judging, feeling inadequate, reviewing the past, or planning for the future — we finally let go of our controlling self-interest and surrender.

People commonly come to this place of surrender after experiencing a dark period of emptiness or suffering, as described by Rabbi David Cooper: "Prior to this moment, the person may feel that all prayers remain unanswered. After conversion [the Christian code word for the enlightenment experience, according to William James], the person experiences . . . a new awareness of infinite light." [22]

This breakthrough into the "infinite light" of unbounded awareness brings an experience of freedom that transforms one's entire process of perception, especially one's perception of oneself. Once you experience that your self is consciousness, and not restricted to the confines of your body, you realize that it is impossible to say where your self ends, and another person's begins. We all overlap. These experiences evoke *understanding* beyond all doubt of our true spiritual nature.

Love of others is the *result* of this self-knowledge, rather than the cause of the knowledge. This love has been characterized by Sri Nisargadatta as "the capacity to enter other focal points of consciousness." The Dalai Lama says that this shared awareness, where we have overcome our mind's isolation, is essential for improving our attitude toward the world, and our relationships with others. We have to know that we are interdependent, and that our best interest is the interest of others. [23]

In Christian literature, the experience of this transforming awareness in which one is filled with love, energy, and light has been called "mystical union," or *"unio mystica"* in Latin. Rabbi David Cooper writes in *The Heart of Stillness* that this experience of illumination and love "marks the pivotal point of an individual's conversion from a sense of separation to a continuous feeling of the presence of the Divine within." [24]

Centering Prayer

Direct experiences of energizing light and spiritual union are not exclusive to Asian traditions. Christianity also has a silent contemplative tradition of "communing with God" without thoughts, words, or emotions. Gregory the Great of the sixth century called it "resting in God." Contemporary Christian scholar Father Thomas Keating of St. Benedict's Monastery in Colorado teaches Centering Prayer as a way to access that resting place in consciousness.

Keating tells us that "resting in God" was the classical meaning of contemplative prayer for the first sixteen centuries after Christ, so this type of silent prayer is not a new idea. His teachings have brought many former Christians back to the church. Many people are drawn to Centering Prayer as a way of healing their addictions or psychological wounds, but recovery or personal healing is not the ultimate goal of this spiritual practice. The goal, according to Keating, is the ability to follow the teachings of Jesus all the way to mystical union. [25]

This prayer is silent and meditative; it is accomplished without the thoughts, words, or emotions that people usually associate with prayer. In Centering Prayer there is neither asking or petitioning for anything, nor pleading with God for mercy or intercession. This prayer of union with God fits with the mystical (inner, experiential) paths of other spiritual teachings.

"God's First Language Is Silence, and Everything Else Is a Bad Translation"

Through Centering Prayer, Father Thomas Keating teaches that a person may embark upon the "spiritual journey" to an experience of self-transcendence and union with the divine. As people develop a regular practice with this type of prayer, he says, the physical, mental, and emotional wounds accumulated over their lifetime rise up from their unconscious mind to their conscious awareness. As these past wounds are gradually brought into awareness, they are silently released through a process called inner purification.

If the wounds of repressed traumas are severe, a person should seek professional counseling to work through them. In any case, people who practice Centering Prayer experience this interior purification as both life-transforming and physically healing. "The level of deep rest accessed during the prayer period loosens up the hardpan around the emotional weeds stored in the unconscious, of which the body seems to be the warehouse," explains Keating. [26]

He teaches that this purification is a necessary process preceding the transformative unfolding of the divine presence within: "God's first language is silence, and everything else is a bad translation! Centering Prayer facilitates a movement into deep interior silence beyond all thoughts, feelings, and sense perceptions. It is a new level beyond words, and becomes a Being to being communication in which the obstacles to greater freedom, creativity, and wholeness are dissolved." [27]

Keating says the "Divine Therapy" that occurs through Centering Prayer differs from the transformation that occurs through meditation. He maintains that meditation focuses one's attention on a repeated mantra, one's breath, or some body sensation as a means of transcending separateness, but union with God is grace, a gift from God. Centering Prayer is silent preparation for that gift, according to Keating, and it is an act of faith that a person does to consent to God's presence and action in his or her life.

With Centering Prayer, a person starts with the *intention* to rest one's consciousness in the presence of God. One reaches union with God through consent, rather than through just letting it happen, or trying to make it happen through concentrating on some *thing*, says

Keating. A simple prayer word, such as "peace," "Jesus," "calm," or "shalom," may be silently repeated to silence any wayward thoughts and to return your intention to awareness of God's presence.

We leave it up to the reader to decide whether there is a significant difference between Centering Prayer and loving-kindness meditation. If a person conceives of God as infinite awareness beyond description, the differences in the transforming experience may not be as great as many Westerners might think.

Keating says that although Centering Prayer is not a tool for developing concentration, releasing stress, or accessing higher states of consciousness, it is consciousness transforming nonetheless, acting as a catalyst for the healthy unloading of our "false self." Our false self, according to Keating, is the needy and driven part of ourselves, the part that feels psychologically wounded, addicted to substances, or inadequate. Our false self is the addictive energy that drives us to invest ourselves in "programs for happiness," to compensate for our "emotional junk of a lifetime."

The dissolution of the false self occurs gradually over time, so a person practicing Centering Prayer can't really judge its effects during a prayer session. The fruits of the spiritual practice are a more joyous and peaceful life; the experience of illumination and union with God may actually emerge later while a person is doing something as simple as flossing her teeth!

The great gift of Keating's work is that he has made a direct experience of God accessible to Christians, many of whom have been previously turning to Eastern meditational practices. Even more important is that Keating has translated classical Christian language into terms that make sense today, in the context of contemporary psychology. He relates such terms as "purgative" and "purification" to the release of, and recovery from, old psychological wounds, resentments, and fears we carry around. Keating's notion of "false self" serves as an equivalent for the traditional concept of "original sin." And "innocence" relates to a state of freedom from "our story," the conscious and unconscious limitations of our past emotional wounds, which block our full awareness of the divine presence within.

To learn more about Centering Prayer, we refer readers to Thomas Keating's books *Open Mind, Open Heart* and *Intimacy with God.*

You Don't Have to Believe Anything to Experience God

According to Keating's teaching, we all have an inherent human potential to be "divinized," the term he says was preferred by the Greek church fathers for the realization of our innate spiritual energy. He reiterates the teaching of other wisdom teachers that this process of spiritual transformation unfolds according to the priority we give it in our lives.

Thomas Keating and Buddhist teachers such as Thich Nhat Hanh provide us with spiritual tool kits to further our opportunity for transcendence in much the same way as the Sutras of Patanjali we described earlier. It is clear that the teachings, whether they be Christian, Buddhist, or Hindu, are all leading us to the same place, although they lead us along different paths. We can all experience God, whatever we call Him, Her, or It, because truth has no boundaries. The Kingdom of God is available to everyone, according to Buddhist monk Thich Nhat Hanh:

> Although God cannot be described by using concepts and notions, that does not mean you cannot experience God the Father. If the wave does not have to die to become water, then we do not have to die to enter the Kingdom of God.
>
> The Kingdom of God is available here and now. The energy of the Holy Spirit is the energy that helps us touch the Kingdom of God. . . . Truth has no boundaries. . . . We hear repeatedly that God is within us. To me, it means that God is within our consciousness. [28]

Addictions and Craving Connectedness

Addiction may be seen as habitually looking to something outside oneself to quell a craving that lies within. Joseph Bailey, author of *The Serenity Principle,* says every addict's primary addiction is to thought. [29] Many psychologists today recognize that addictive cravings, whatever their biological bases, are also a substitute for transpersonal, beyond-the-self experiences. We all have a natural inclination to want to feel a meaningful connection to something greater than our separate selves.

A 1998 survey of teenagers' attitudes conducted by the *New York Times* and CBS News found that 39 percent of our country's youth claimed that drug abuse was the biggest problem facing their generation. [30] Carl Jung described such cravings for addictive substances, in a letter to the founder of Alcoholics Anonymous, as "the equivalent, on a low level, of the spiritual thirst of our being for wholeness. . . . " He explained that our concept of wholeness was characterized as "union with God" in medieval language. [31]

Jung recognized that recovery from addiction was facilitated by religious *experience,* or some similar "higher education of the mind beyond the confines of mere rationalism." [32] This is one reason why Alcoholics Anonymous, with its emphasis on a connection to some power beyond the confines of one's separate mind, is so successful in addiction's rehabilitation.

Alcoholics and addicts aren't the only people craving meaningful spirituality in their lives, however. In a 1997 Gallup Institute poll of Americans' feelings concerning death, the issues people worried about most were spiritual — not monetary or accomplishment-related. [33] Only about one third of the people surveyed who hoped for spiritual comfort in their final days thought clergy would provide it. And while half of all the people polled consider prayer important at life's end, they feared they would die feeling cut off from a higher power.

Those addicted to shopping, eating, sex, and house remodeling may also crave a feeling of connection, of meaning, and the accompanying peace that transpersonal experiences bring. Essayist Lewis Lapham suggested in the *Wall Street Journal* that Americans express their longing for the spiritually ineffable in the wolfishness of their appetites. For people who seek to quell their unnamable angst and unending desires with buying and owning things, the "feasts of consumption become rituals of communion." [34] The best-selling book *Your Money or Your Life* tells us, "Consumption seems to be our favorite high, our nationally sanctioned addiction, the all-American form of substance abuse." [35]

Many of us seek meaningful spiritual experiences, but feel alienated by the dogmas, creeds, rituals, and forms of institutionalized religions. People do think prayer — the experience of a relationship with some higher power — is important, but they are unfamiliar with it.

Prayer Is an Altered State of Consciousness

Prayer is an altered state of consciousness, because our attention is not focused on any *thing*, action, or conscious thought. Our mind is quiet, our attention directed inward instead of outward — in itself an unusual state of consciousness. Carl Jung wrote, "In the history of the collective, as in the history of the individual, everything depends on the development of consciousness." [36] Christian mystic Teilhard de Chardin knew that "evolution is an ascent towards consciousness," echoing what his contemporary Sri Aurobindo in India expressed: "A change of consciousness is the major fact of the next evolutionary transformation. . . . An evolution of consciousness is the central motive of terrestrial existence." [37]

All these great minds believed that part of our mission as humans is to develop and refine our consciousness, and to take control of our minds. When we do this, we will begin to realize that whatever we experience from moment to moment is highly dependent upon how we choose to focus our attention. Anything we can attain is already part of our essential nature. Entry into the spiritual dimension is not the birth of a new being, as Richard Bucke thought in 1901, but an awakening to who we already are.

Liberation from the Self

Albert Einstein believed it was an "optical delusion of our consciousness" that we experienced ourselves — our thoughts and feelings — as separated from each other. He said this delusion was related to our misperception of space and time, and that our task must be to free ourselves from the prison of our illusion of separateness. Today's philosophers are finally exploring the paths out of our prison of illusion that Einstein recognized and wrote about: "The true value of a human being is determined primarily by the measure and the sense in which he has attained liberation from the self." [38]

With similar scientific thinking, astrophysicist Sir Arthur Eddington said that our minds only seemed separate because of "the narrow limits of our particular consciousness. . . . " [39] And more recently, physicist David Bohm has written of our "quantum interconnectedness."

The mid-twentieth-century Christian mystic and spiritual healer Joel Goldsmith wrote over thirty books on a state of awareness he characterized as connection with the infinite and called "practicing the presence." He said simply that prayer is a state of receptivity in which truth is realized without conscious thought. His definition didn't mention God, or ask for anything from anyone. He said God could not be seen, understood, known, or explained with the human intellect. God could be *experienced* as an activity in consciousness, but not through thinking or doing anything. He taught that God could only be discerned through a "spiritual sense." He emphasized that "In most cases it is a *developed* sense, and we must *consciously* develop it." [40]

Now, consciously developing a spiritual sense, in order to experience an activity in our consciousness, sounds very much like the "evolution of consciousness," referred to by Chardin and Aurobindo. Thus, one clear reason for a person to explore prayer is to develop this intuitive sense, which cannot be accessed with the intellect or experienced with the senses.

All wisdom teachers have said that the commitment to one's evolution of consciousness is a self-selecting process. They also say that the experience of personal suffering creates the readiness. We usually consider prayer when desperately hoping to overcome an illness, but spiritual healers argue that illness can *initiate* a consciousness of the infinite. However, meditation and meditative prayer are tools of consciousness, whether or not you are suffering or ill. We don't have to be sick to get better. We also don't have to embrace the dogma of any particular religion in order to have spirituality in our lives.

You Don't Have to Be Religious

Another reason someone might want to pray comes from physician and author Herbert Benson, professor of medicine at Harvard Medical School and developer of the health-promoting and mind-quieting Relaxation Response discussed in the previous chapter. After more than twenty-five years experience as a researcher and physician, Benson concluded that we are not only nourished by transpersonal experiences such as prayer and meditation but indeed "wired for God." He explains in his book *Timeless Healing:*

> Studies . . . have persuaded me that, coincidentally or by divine decree, humans do have a universal, physical propensity for faith. At our core, we are all organisms sustained and nourished by life-affirming beliefs and philosophies. We are designed to flex spiritual muscles, even if our prayers are very different, even if we don't call it prayer.
>
> Scattered across the globe, people have said prayers and meditations that evoked physical calm. . . . No matter how confused our languages, no matter how distinct our cultures and creeds, we share innate gifts — of physical healing, of achieving peace, and sometimes of feeling "the presence of a power or energy force which feels near." [41]

So we might also want to "flex spiritual muscles" to achieve better health, greater peace, and an experience of energy not otherwise accessible. But to whom would I pray, you may ask, if I don't believe in the bearded man in the sky — if I don't believe there is *anyone* to pray to?

Who Is God?

In response to this eternal question, the eleventh-century mystic St. Anselm wrote, "God is that, the greater than which cannot be conceived." To Spinoza and Einstein, God was an "organizing principle of the universe"; to Hegel, "Absolute Spirit"; to Martin Buber, "The Eternal Thou"; to Paul Tillich, "The Ground of Our Being" and "Ultimate Reality." To St. Catherine of Siena, God was "Pure Love." God was "The Eternal Light" to Dante, "The Energetic Word" to St. Bernard, "The One" to Plotinus, as well as the "Supplier of True Life," and "His Majesty" to St. Teresa of Avila, and "That Which Is" to St. Augustine.

Great Spirit, the Tao, the Beloved, Ein Sof, Brahman, Divine Mother, I Am, Yahweh, Infinite Absolute, First Cause, Life Force, Source, Infinite Consciousness, or even your Higher Self — can you relate to any of these ideas of God? Reading this far, you might be able to conceive of God as the limitless, nonlocal mind in which our consciousness is embedded.

Remember that Joel Goldsmith said God, or Truth, was beyond comprehension, but could be experienced as an activity in one's consciousness. Sanskrit scholar Ernest Wood said God was a good word if we remember that it is a word of discovery, like a boat in which we set sail to discover something we don't know — a word to give direction to the mind, rather than a definition. [42] Or, as in the title of Rabbi David Cooper's recent book, "God is a verb." In the realm of oneness and no-thing-ness of divine union, spirit dissolves all distinctions. As John Blofeld has said, in a dimension "where space and form are transcended and we are considering an invisible, omnipresent source of blessedness, the difference between a being and a state of being is obviously hard to define." [43]

Hardwired for God?

Benson concluded that belief in something boundless and limitless is natural to humanity. Every culture he studied had religious or secular practices that consisted of two basic steps: (1) a repetitive or stabilizing focus of attention, and (2) a passive attitude toward intrusive thoughts. In other words, don't resist thoughts, don't judge them, and don't react to them. Just stay relaxed and notice them as they flow by in your stream of consciousness.

All around the world, and in every culture, these two aspects are part of practices that calm the mind — *and* transform consciousness and promote healing. Benson encountered multitudes of descriptions for this peaceful state. So you might think of prayer as something you do with your mind that keeps your attention focused without thinking, and brings you an experience of peace.

In all the years Benson spent teaching people to quiet their mind, he found that focusing attention on some "greatness beyond which there can be nothing greater," whether or not a person believed in God *per se,* evoked the greatest calm and healing. Focusing on some boundless and limitless essential principle of the universe that includes and surpasses humanity was the most effective way for his patients to quiet their minds.

This boundless and limitless essential principle that brings people peace reminds us of the words of an unknown medieval author, who said, "God may well be loved but not thought." *A Course in Miracles* teaches that love is joining, with no barriers of separation, and the Vedanta master Sri Nisargadatta said love is the refusal to separate. [44] Ramana Maharshi taught that the experience of not forgetting consciousness alone is the state of devotion or *bhakti*, which is the relationship of unfading real love. [45]

Nisargadatta taught in his inspiring book *I Am That* that in order to know God, or the Self, one should, "Refuse all thoughts except one: the thought 'I am.' The mind will rebel in the beginning, but with patience and perseverance it will yield. Once you are quiet, things will happen spontaneously and naturally, without any interference on your part." [46]

This sounds very much like the Bible's words, "Be still, and know that I am God" and "I am that I am" (Exodus 3:16). Actually, many Biblical scholars believe that Jesus knew of Vedantic wisdom. Many of his teachings are quite similar: "Before Abraham was, I am." (John 8:58) "I and my father are one." (John 10:30) "The kingdom of God is within you." (Luke 17:21) "I am with you always. . . . " (Matthew 28:20) What is meant by "I am that I am" is that nothing exists outside the universal mind, when It is not being limited by ego's thoughts of separateness. God is therefore pure, undiluted awareness Itself.

Advaita Vedanta — The Truth of Not Two

Vedanta wisdom derives from the Vedas, the oldest records of Asian wisdom, dating back at least 3,500 years, which were later canonized by Hindus. In 1893, these teachings were first brought to the West by Swami Vivekananda, the disciple of Sri Ramakrishna. Vedanta became known to a wider circle of Westerners who traveled to India in the first half of the twentieth century to study with another revered Indian saint, Sri Ramana Maharshi.

Advaita means "not two," or nondual. The Advaita Vedantic view of reality is that there exists eternally only one infinite consciousness, and in reality, you and I are this consciousness; it is our true self. Vedantic realization is the direct and immediate experience that you are neither the body nor the mind, but limitless consciousness. Happiness, peace, joy, love, and a sense of expansiveness and freedom are the natural by-products of these self-revelations. These manifestations of a spiritual life are obviously similar to those of Christian teachings.

Vedanta teaches that we are not our bodies, and our bodies do not produce our awareness. Instead, we are that which is *aware* of forms and bodies. We are consciousness, and "Consciousness and Existence are inseparable. Existence is aware, and Awareness is eternally existing." [47] In Vedanta, "existence" is another name for God, and we are that existence. The Catholic Saint Francis shared at least one idea of the Vedas. In describing the goal of the spiritual quest, he said, "What we are looking for is who is looking." If you have ever wondered if you really exist, close your eyes, direct your attention within, and ask yourself, "Who wants to know?"

The power of asking "Who wants to know?" as a way of knowing God is called self-inquiry. Vedanta teachers say that all religious practices for knowing God are postponements, because no ritual or activity will bring you closer to what you already are. The teacher Gangaji describes self-inquiry as "an intense concentration of attention on the *source* of this attention and awareness itself." [48] The method is to close your eyes, and focus on the source of your attention, asking yourself, "Who am I?" Ask also, "Who is aware of this body? Who is aware of these sensory impressions, images, and thoughts?"

Who Wants to Know? — Knowing God Through Self-Inquiry

To perform the process of self-inquiry, your must withdraw your attention from anything outside yourself: any object, or even your body. The goal is to let your mind rest in its source. Other meditation methods teach you to focus your attention on some thing: an object, breath, *chakra* or energy center. This approach is different because its focus is the subject, the meditator, *you.* It also recognizes that you, the one asking, are an already existing reality right now, that no goal is to be achieved in the future. "The fact that one wave real-

izes that it is part of the Ocean does not change anything in totality.
. . . One Infinite Consciousness exists as it is always." [49] We, as waves,
were never separate from the ocean of consciousness.

A second variant of self-inquiry is to direct your attention to the
sense of beingness, or the "I am" feeling. In order to focus on the feeling of existence, a person is advised to repeat inwardly, "I, I, I," and
to try to intimately feel where in the body this inner sound comes
from. Ramana Maharshi experienced that this inner feeling of existence emanated from an area above the chest, about two finger-
widths to the right of center. He called this our spiritual heart center,
but said it had no form, and we should keep our attention on the
inner feeling of beingness, and not on any location in the body or
elsewhere.

Igor Kungurtsev, author of *Advaitic Realization,* teaches that if
we sit and dedicate all our attention and all our love to "I am" and
the inner feeling of "I," and if we disregard all distracting thoughts,
images, and sensations, the feeling of our individual separate "I" will
dissolve, and "vast formless Existence will reveal Itself." [50] And
according to Vedanta, this existence is consciousness itself.

Vedanta teaches that an experiential discovery of one's essence as
infinite consciousness is immediately available to all sincere seekers of
any religious persuasion who persevere in search of truth. Ramana
Maharshi became enlightened at the age of seventeen through self-
inquiry. He was not exclusively a Hindu; he did not practice any rituals, and though many of his followers were Christian and Muslim,
he never recommended they change religions. Maharshi taught that
the purpose of all religious scriptures was to "make a man retrace his
steps to his original source," a similar idea to the Christian concept
of "resting in God."

All of the world's great spiritual traditions talk of transitory flash-
es of great insight or illumination that appear unexpectedly and then

fade away, leaving the percipient with the certainty that one's usual state of awareness is severely limited and misleading. The religions of the world all describe methods for attaining and maintaining an altered state of expanded awareness. They all describe goals of extending and stabilizing these transcendent states of awareness, and they all have names for these extended states — salvation, *samadhi,* liberation, enlightenment, the Kingdom of God, deification, self-realization, *wu,* and *mukti* — all referring to awakening, freedom, and release into ultimate consciousness.

These altered states are life-transforming — physically, mentally, emotionally, and behaviorally. They improve health and enhance perceptions and understanding. We realize with certainty our essential interconnection with all of life at the level of consciousness. Through this deep knowing that we are not separate, life takes on new meaning, and we become more peaceful, happy, and compassionate. Life goals shift. We seek to further refine our capacity for accessing this loving, energizing state of awareness, and we form a desire to help others to learn to do the same.

Prayer is available for us to expand our awareness. In this universe of nonlocal mind, when one thing changes, everything changes. Our power lies in changing ourselves — changing our minds — and in doing so, elevating the consciousness of the world.

We have all read and heard that awakened beings are very rare in the world. This may have been true in the past, but whether or not this continues to be true in the present and future is up to us, now. The light of pure awareness is available to illumine quiet minds. In the following chapter we address the question, "Where is the attention that you call your life?"

The Heart of the Mind

The Essential First Steps toward Gratitude and Forgiveness

*We are dragon fire. We are the creative, scintil-
lating, searing, healing flame of the awesome
and enchanting universe.*

— Brian Swimme
The Universe Is a Green Dragon

When they asked us what we wanted to be when we grew up, they really meant, "What do you want to *do?*" Whatever we might have chosen, it was not the same as choosing what or how to *be*. "Let the beauty of what you love be what you do," the Sufi mystic Rumi said in the thirteenth century. Be beauty, as artists painting the canvas of their lives. Be love.

But how? In today's world, most people understandably look to their jobs to define themselves. Having found no meaningful spirituality, they assume their work will adequately fill the traditional role of religion, as an aid in answering the questions, "Who am I?" and "Why am I here?"

We all want to lead happy, fulfilled, and meaningful lives. These goals are universal, even though very different things bring different people happiness. For some, fulfillment is attained through raising a family, earning money, or playing sports; for others, it may appear in writing, cooking, or artistic expression. And we all want to be loved.

Eastern wisdom traditions teach that because our thoughts, feelings, and desires are constantly changing, we will never achieve enduring happiness or peace of mind through objects, relationships, or anything outside ourselves. Things wear out, get lost, fall out of fashion, or break. The person in our perfect relationship turned out not to be who we thought they were. And then *we* turn out not to be who we thought we were. Each of us is an ever-changing series of events, interpreted through our, and other people's, hopelessly subjective perspectives. We simply won't find the ultimate meaning of life in another ever-changing person.

Our minds are always wandering, reacting to other people's behaviors and words, and taken over by the thoughts and memories streaming through our awareness. So it is also fruitless to seek lasting happiness through thought, or even through sensual pleasures. What attracts us today fails to satisfy tomorrow. Yet we continue to think that serenity comes from something we do or have, rather than the way we are.

Really, we are all seeking a relatively satisfied and stable state of mind, free of cravings or fears. Eastern philosophies call the inner feeling of enduring calm and causeless joy resulting from union with God "bliss." They distinguish inner bliss from Western societies' concepts of pleasure or happiness — fleeting feelings that focus on temporary bodily sensations, acquiring *things,* or changing circumstances to satisfy our desires.

According to Eastern thought, the reason we feel good after buying a new car, or eating a delicious chocolate, or having great sex, is that our cravings and graspings are temporarily silenced. We mistake this momentary pleasure for freedom and peace of mind, and so we hunt for more objects, experiences, or accomplishments to fix our inner craving for wholeness. We search for security, position, pleasure, and comfort when we should be searching for truth.

This inner, instinctual search — a search for God — is inborn in all people. Eastern philosophy teaches we will never be satisfied until we become still— until we stop moving, doing, thinking, remodeling, and attending to outer sensations, and start listening within. A divine plan is unfolding, and when our soul is ready, we'll participate.

For centuries, the Bible has presented its message that religion is an experience in consciousness. Unfortunately, people memorize its prayers and promises instead of seeking that experience. In this lifetime, we have the opportunity to consciously create a receptive state within our mind to commune with infinite consciousness. Belonging or not belonging to a church or religion, and performing or not performing spiritual rituals has little to do with a person's relationship with God, or spiritual consciousness. Although the human mind creates desire and then fulfills it, wisdom traditions tell us our deep longing for truth and freedom is our soul's yearning to experience its boundless depths. The stream of consciousness we each call "my life" is the universal journey of infinite consciousness or God awakening to itself. It is this consciousness that informs and animates each of us.

Consciousness discovering itself, by way of you and me — what could that possibly mean? Spiritual master Yogananda said that because the ultimate motive for people's actions is the attainment of spiritual happiness or bliss, our very existence is bound up with this innate goal. This fundamental and universal motive may be seen as our true religion, or "that which binds us," which is the original meaning of the word religion, from the Latin *religare*. It follows that whatever *actions* we take to satisfy our yearning for inner happiness and peace may be called "religious," whether or not they have anything to do with organized religions' creeds or systems of belief. [1] Whatever you do to experience inner peace, connectedness, and meaning is your religion.

You may or may not presently feel bound by religious beliefs. You may have already ascertained that truth based on one individual's direct experience will have difficulty surviving in any religious organization. Organizations are headed by people, and people with inherently different experience and beliefs will have conflicting ideas about the truth of other people's revelations.

Each of us must discover our religion for ourselves. This book is about the transcendent experience that is available to all of us, the experience spiritual masters throughout history have tried to describe. This experience transforms a person's perceptions of life so profoundly that organized religions devise sets of rules they think will bring others to the same experience. If you have read this far, you are probably a seeker who suspects that spiritual transformation is *possible,* but who may be repelled by the dogma and rituals you encounter in religious services.

You *can* have a spiritual life, without having to go anywhere, or believe anything. You do, however, have to "show up for God," and pay attention, just as you do when you want to build a relationship with another person. It's simple, but it takes practice, and patience.

We Create Ourselves by How We Invest Our Attention

Everything we experience in our lives depends on our conscious awareness. Think about it. If you want to experience something different, you have to focus your attention on something different. Most people take a trip, buy a new toy, or seek a new partner to divert their attention.

Enduring peace and happiness, or the more all-encompassing "bliss," is an internal condition, so it can't be acquired through objects or circumstances outside ourselves. It is a state of mind at rest — undisturbed by thoughts, imaginings, desires, or fears. To the quiet mind, ruffling waves of thought come and go, but our attention remains undisturbed. Inside our mind is spacious, full awareness. Once experienced, this inner stillness of effortless attention itself *transforms* the mind. We begin to perceive everything differently.

Repeated experiences of that stillness, according to numerous spiritual masters, bring increased physical and mental well-being, clarity of thought and insight, spontaneous joy, and loving feelings with no particular cause. You may have heard that the quality of your attention is the greatest gift you can give anyone. The quality of our pure attention is also the greatest gift we can give our *true* selves — the part of us that never changes.

Through the transformative experience, one's awareness expands to include an overwhelming sense of connectedness with others — a state of being that people describe as intensely loving, but of no one in particular. This love seems timeless, without relation to appearances. Each moment of loving expands to become a timeless *now* without duration. Such an experience of oneness with this consciousness is a feeling of being loved and *being love* all at the same time. This is what is so transforming.

Repeated experiences with this awareness may also enhance the psychic abilities we've discussed in previous chapters, but that is not the purpose of seeking the experience. The direct experience of interconnected consciousness with others is far more intense and compelling. This spiritual transformation of consciousness from separation to unity is the development of wisdom.

Such wisdom is gained by allowing one's individual mind to do something that has been called a variety of things by different traditions: letting your mind "rest in its source," or "consenting to the presence of the Holy Spirit," "join or rest with God," "enter the void," or simply "attain *satori.*" In each concept, some spiritual aspect of ourselves joins some consciousness greater than our separate mind. A powerful force is generated by directing your attention inward and maintaining that state. This creates a transcendent experience, which promotes wisdom, or even enlightenment.

All faiths teach that you can't see transformed consciousness in a person by looking; it only appears in a person's way of being: in kindness, spontaneous joy, generosity, and inner tranquillity in the midst of confusion. Such people lead their lives immanently aware of our interconnected consciousness. This awareness allows them to effortlessly share in the others' happiness, and appreciate others' good deeds.

These ways of being share an *understanding* that comes from a person's *direct experience* of a dimension of life that extends beyond ordinary humanhood. The experience of oneness transforms human consciousness in a way that codified religious rules of conduct never can. A person's actions spring from a sense of loving and giving, rather than from the more ordinary human strategies of defending, competing, and getting.

Buddhist teacher Sylvia Boorstein says that compassion is the natural response of the heart when unclouded by our specious assumption that we are separate from one another. [2] She writes that traditional texts describe compassion as "the quivering of the heart" in resonance or coherence with someone else's feelings. It's a *feeling* of oneness, not just an idea of how one ought to feel. This quivering is subtle, and requires a quiet mind.

Jesus gave *spiritual* significance to only two commandments when asked, "Master, which *is* the great commandment in the law?" (Matthew 22:36). Compassion was one of them: "You shall love your neighbor as yourself." (Matthew 22:37–38) He compared this commandment to the one He said was his first and greatest: "You shall love the Lord your God with all your heart, and with all your soul, and with *all your mind.* On these two commandments hang *all* the law and the prophets." (Mat 22:38–40; Mark 12:30–31) Our mind includes our attention, certainly, and loving involves joining, or removing psychic barriers of separation. So consciously "joining one's mind with God" might involve loving God with all one's mind. And we are told that this occurs in quiet: "Be still, and know that I am God." (Psalm 46:10)

Nowhere did Jesus say it was necessary to go to church, or believe Bible stories to experience God. But He did clarify how we would know if someone understood His teachings: "By this shall all men know that ye are my disciples, if ye have love one to another." (John 13:35)

In joining minds with God, or unbounded consciousness, it is necessary to empty one's mind of self-centered ideas, to allow it to fill with a dimension of awareness that transcends human thought. Historically, letting one's mind align with the active source of awareness or the life force has been called prayer; what we do in silent preparation for that joining has been known as meditation. As long as prayers are filled with words, thoughts, hopes, fears, pleadings, suggestions, or outlines for God to follow, we are actually praying to our *own* mind, not infinite mind. Such petitionary or intercessory prayers may also be effective, but a receptive mind is necessary to apprehend transcendent consciousness, because prayer is a way of going outside the human ego to effect change.

Different Attentions, Different Realities

Directing our attention to joining our mind with the mind of God is one way of applying what psychologist Mihaly Csikszentmihalyi meant when he said that our attention is our most important tool for improving the quality of our life experience. "We create ourselves by how we invest the energy of our attention," he wrote. We create our life experiences, and ourselves, by what we notice and pay attention to. He also said that *entirely different realities will emerge depending on how we invest our attention.* When we focus the energy of our *intention* on aligning our separate mind with infinite consciousness, we transform our individual mind and we recreate ourselves.

For millennia, spiritual masters have maintained that the root of all suffering is the belief the we are separate from each other, and from the source of our consciousness. Vedanta teacher Sri Nisargadatta emphasizes:

> To know what you are, you must first investigate and know what you are not.
>
> Discover all that you are not — body, feelings, thoughts, time, space, this or that — nothing . . . which you perceive can be you. The very act of perceiving shows that you are not what you perceive. [3]

The Heart of the Mind

In the transformation of consciousness that the Catholic mystic Teilhard de Chardin and the Indian spiritual leader Aurobindo described as our evolutionary mandate in Chapter 6, a person's awareness expands beyond his or her separate mind to encompass a connection and unity with infinite consciousness. This is the experience of the heart of the mind.

This experience of unity consciousness may be accompanied by physiological sensations akin to one's heart bursting with love. But consciously deciding to end one's personal suffering, and helping others to experience this transformation is the greatest joy, according to Vedanta teacher Gangaji:

> If you end mental fixation on personal problems, awakening of Self to Itself is served. Your life is then naturally used to facilitate the awakening of all being. Service to awakening is discovered to be the deepest bliss." [4]

The recognition that we are spiritual beings interconnected in consciousness is "love." It is universal, with no cause, object, or personal agenda. Nisargadatta Maharaj talked of this interconnection when he said that love is the capacity to enter other focal points of consciousness. The direct experience that we are all connected, and part of God, has been called "self-realization" or "awakening" in various Asian traditions, and referred to as "conversion" or being filled with "Christ Consciousness" in Christian traditions. No particular spiritual path has a monopoly on achieving oneness with God, and with everyone else.

Surrender What?

Surrender means relinquishing the human sense of isolation and separation. Surrender does not mean "giving in"; it means being willing "to see differently," beyond the masks of suffering we all wear. It is an act of humility, in which we give our need to control things over to a force greater than ourselves. It means giving up the control, *not* the caring; it means giving up the aggression, the protection, the justification, and the defenses that come from one's limited perspective.

Surrender means ceasing the activity of the restless, reactive, judging mind, in order to allow a quiet open space in one's consciousness. It means detaching from our desire for particular outcomes. It means choosing inner peace as our goal instead of being right, and consciously directing one's energy toward resolving the conflict instead of continuing the struggle.

Surrender is liberating, but it does not bring the liberation *of* an individual person — it brings liberation *from* the sense of individual separateness. It unclutters the mind, and creates an expansive inner stillness, unbounded by fear or defensiveness. It frees a person to act from a natural loving state, instead of from self-protection. Spiritual consciousness doesn't work *for* us — it works *in* and *through* us, and transforms open human minds. This surrender is to the truth of who we are — an acceptance of our interdependence.

So How Do I Get My Mind to Mind?

The most powerful way of directing our mind to change our life experience, is to let it become still, so that it empties itself of all thoughts! To experience the heart of the mind, and access its transcendent inner state of well-being, we must first realize that it is possible for us to take control of our thoughts, instead of being unconsciously controlled *by* them. Then a person must appreciate that refining one's awareness is worthwhile. Lastly, a person must deeply desire a new way of being — a transformation of perception.

Many books and teachers from a variety of spiritual traditions offer methods on how to manage your mind or how to practice particular religions. In the previous chapter, we discussed different spiritual approaches that we have found helpful, including Centering Prayer, Buddhist meditation, and Self-Inquiry, and we list sources that have inspired us in the bibliography. In addition, we hold dear two classics that give clear, effective lessons for transforming one's life through changing attitudes and thoughts: *Love Is Letting Go of Fear* by Dr. Gerald Jampolsky, and *Change Your Mind, Change Your Life* by Jampolsky and his wife Diane Cirincione.[5] These books give understandable instructions on how to "choose peace instead of being right." Author Hugh Prather wrote in the foreword to *Love Is Letting Go of Fear,* "There must be another way to go through life besides being pulled through it kicking and screaming." Jampolsky's books describe another way.

The guidelines offered in these books for shifting perceptions and choosing what we want to experience have been named "Attitudinal Healing," because they teach how to let go of the compulsion to judge, condemn, and control others; how to adopt the life goal of peace of mind; and how to open our heart to feel whole and loving again.

Choosing Peace as the Goal through Forgiveness

Jampolsky's books are both based on the lessons in *A Course in Miracles,* a self-study course of spiritual psychotherapy that teaches how to remove obstacles to peace in one's life.[6] The books describe how to transform fear, anger, guilt, and blame into opportunities for personal transformation. Through this process, difficulties in rela-tionships with people we dislike become opportunities for learning, instead of constant hassles. Primary among the lessons is that when a person chooses peaceful-mindedness as the main goal, the method for achieving that goal is *forgiveness*. In addition to changing the way we think and react, Jampolsky and Cirincione stress the importance of quieting the mind and following inner spiritual guidance as essen-tial components of their program for finding peace.

Forgiveness doesn't mean deciding that what everyone does is okay. It has nothing to do with justice, condoning, or excusing. In a nutshell, *A Course in Miracles* says that forgiveness is undoing the decision to blame. The purpose of forgiveness is to free your own mind, so as not to let someone else's *past* behavior control your *pre-sent* experience. Forgiveness means unhooking our attention from the past, stopping our projection of painful past experiences into our future, refraining from cluttering our mind with ongoing judgments and criticisms about people, and maintaining our awareness in the present.

Forgiveness allows us to act, instead of react; it clears our focus so we can experience peace in the present moment. The present is actually the only place where peace can be experienced! So to have more peace in our lives, we have to expand our awareness of the suc-cession of present moments we call our life.

Forgiveness is an antidote to what psychologist Csikszentmihalyi calls "psychic disorder." Psychic disorder occurs when our attention is diverted with information that conflicts with, or distracts us from, our intentions. We experience psychic disorder as pain, fear, resent-ment, anxiety, or jealousy. Ongoing psychic disorder creates distress and depression, so each of us has to pay attention to the contents of our own mind; we need to stop seeking justification for our mental suffering in the actions of others.

Psychic disorder is related to what Jampolsky and Cirincione term "the split mind." Our ability to forgive heals our own split minds. It is the magic ingredient that allows us to give up the personal wars we are fighting within. When our personal wars are ended, our lives are no longer limited to the personal — they turn toward peace and reconciliation in the world.

Forgiveness frees our attention, and enables us to *be present* in the present, which is where *all* our experiences really take place. *A Course in Miracles* says forgiveness breaks the cycle of time by leaving the past behind. Similarly, the Dalai Lama suggests that carrying hatred around in our hearts makes us what our enemies are. In this sense, forgiveness protects us from being conquered by hatred itself. It's a form of inner disarmament and liberation.

Forgiveness is also an important tool for transcendence, because it allows us to clear space in our mind for God. It paves the way for unobstructed communion with infinite consciousness, because it's easier to clear your mind of wayward thoughts when past resentments and worries aren't floating around in your mindstream. When a person decides that a quiet mind of inner peace is the most important goal, forgiveness will soon follow. And forgiveness is the greatest gift you can give yourself.

Other lessons from *A Course in Miracles* in Jampolsky and Cirincione's books are that, in terms of consciousness, there are only two forms of communication: expressions of love, or the joining of minds, and expressions of fear, which create separations of mind. Expressions of *fear,* which can appear as anger, guilt, blame, jealousy, and resentment, are actually *calls for love and joining.* In the absence of fear, our minds are naturally joined in a consciousness of unity, called love. When you perceive other people's attacks as calls for love, it's much easier not to return the attack — to choose peace and transformation of your consciousness as your goal, instead of being right.

Without Necessity, There Is No Action

The desire for spiritual truth and transformation must endure beyond day-to-day mood swings. Wisdom teachers throughout history have repeated that we are the vehicles of personal and global consciousness transformation. They continue to invite us to claim our privilege, power, and responsibility as cocreators of the universe. But we have to decide that the transformation is necessary, because as Yogananda taught, "Without necessity, there is no action." The world doesn't really need new teachings; it needs new experience. Those of us privileged enough to be free of worry about our immediate survival and safety have the opportunity to live our lives from the question, "How can I be used?" We don't have to know how — we can live our lives discovering how, starting with the intention to be helpful.

Author and spiritual teacher Marianne Williamson declares that we are each called to make a conscious lifestyle decision: "Our life is either continued fuel for the status quo," she writes, "which is a crumbling, overly materialistic order, or our life energies are midwives in the labor room of the higher selves now trying to be born within our species." [7]

To pray, according to Williamson, is to recognize that we have the power to use the laws of consciousness. Passively assuming that God's will is done is not at all the same as *choosing* to bring forth God's truth on this planet. She says the truth of God is behind a veil, and with prayer we reweave the fabric of the universe. "Prayer is going back to the will of the Father so it becomes expressed in our life," she writes. [8] Williamson advocates all types of prayer, but reiterates that the highest form of prayer is not an entreaty but simply knowing that we are one with God. The question isn't how we pray; it is whether we do it at all.

Our Self-Perception Determines Our Behavior

Whether or not we choose to recognize our potential, and what we choose to focus our attention on are aspects of free will. *A Course in Miracles* reminds us that our behavior is determined by our self-perception. What we choose to do is based on who we think we are. You may previously have thought that you are just a body, having life for a time. In that case, your life's attention may have been primarily directed toward bodies and things.

Our purpose in writing this book is to present the idea that we are spiritual beings having a body for a time, and that expansion of our awareness and transformation of consciousness are possible. These are obviously not new ideas; we've just tried to present them in clear English, relatively free of doctrinal language. Our seemingly separate minds are actually imbedded in a sea of infinite consciousness, unbounded by space or time. Our minds are transducers of spiritual consciousness, expressing itself through our individual mind-stream.

Spiritual consciousness never reveals itself as power over people. It reveals itself as *service unto* people. Its transforming nature is revealed through people's *qualities,* or their *ways of being,* more than *what* they do, or which psychic abilities they demonstrate. Each of us can choose to develop these qualities within ourselves, and expand our awareness and potential by consciously opening our mind channels to truth, or what Einstein called, "The Organizing Principle of the Universe." It matters not whether we conceive of the principle as a Divine Father or Mother, or as Great Spirit, Love, Brahman, or Nonlocal Mind. We can open our awareness to it, and experience its activity in our consciousness. As Sylvia Boorstein says, "Waking up is nonsectarian." 9

The Kingdom of God Is Still Within

We are all aware of how religious leaders and institutions throughout history have used the concept of "God is on *our* side" for the dissemination of fear and condemnation, political tyranny, and genocide. Despite this treacherous history, often in the name of organized religions, each of us is nevertheless capable of accessing an intimate connection with infinite consciousness, and activating our innate power to bring light into the world. We *can* know God without believing anything.

Jesus revealed the way to know God when he said, "The kingdom of God cometh not with observation: Neither shall they say, Lo here! Or lo there! . . . The kingdom of God is within you!" (Luke 17:20–21) We don't need holy temples, holy churches, holy doctrines, holy mountains, holy prayers, or even holy teachers. Moses, Elijah, Isaiah, Patanjali, Shankara, Jesus, John, Buddha, Lao-tse, Ramakrishna, Ramana Maharshi, Krishnamurti, Sai Baba, Mother Teresa, and countless others have always told us that their truth came from their experience. The function of spiritual masters is to serve — to serve as examples for those who have not yet realized their true identity. They all tell us that truth is revealed by truth itself, through faculties within our own consciousness, not by human beings through words and thoughts of the mind.

As Gangaji writes, "When I say trust your Self, I mean to trust the truth of who you are. For this trust to be complete, you must first discover who you are. You cannot wait any longer, and you cannot rely on someone else's interpretation — mine, your parents', or your government's. You have to discover directly who you are." [10]

Many people begin a spiritual search to find personal happiness, or to end personal suffering. Their search springs from a desire for personal improvement, or to acquire something, such as health or enlightenment. In reality, enlightenment is the realization that no person exists separate from another. And if enlightenment is liberation from one's sense of separation, then true prayer is beyond words or thoughts; it is the yearning for spiritual awakening for all. Preoccupation with personal gain becomes a willingness to be an instrument of help in lifting the world toward higher consciousness.

As to whether one person can make a difference here, we should remember that Moses, Buddha, and Jesus all did very well. And Joel Goldsmith taught that most people who have attained any degree of spiritual stature were unknown before they became enlightened. It is only the inspiration they experienced, and the love they expressed, that made them more than nobodies to the rest of us.

As for how to experience God, Mother Teresa left a map. She said:

> The Fruit of Silence is Prayer;
> [*First comes silence*, which leads to an experience of oneness];
> The Fruit of Prayer is Faith;
> [Faith is a knowing, derived from experience];
> The Fruit of Faith is Love;
> [The direct experience of unity consciousness brings a knowing
>   that we are connected];
> The Fruit of Love is Service;
> [Giving comes from the understanding that we are not separate;
> Love extends itself through us];
> The Fruit of Service is Peace.
> [The world changes as we are changed.]

Gratitude Is the Gearshift

So transformation all comes down to stopping our runaway thoughts? What about all our good ideas? Stop them too? How, when we've spent all our lives cultivating them? The gearshift we use to downshift our minds is gratitude, crowding out the other chatter with loving thoughts of appreciation.

One grateful thought changes everything. Even the smallest gratitude for the most insubstantial thing halts the suffering within. The most contracted and intense fear and anger are transformed by focusing attention on memories of the heart instead of memories of the mind.

When you become so upset that you can't turn off the distressing thoughts, you can say to yourself, "I choose peace, instead of this. I surrender my suffering. I let go of my story. I end my war within." Then try to remember one wonderful sensation that you have experienced in your past: one delicious taste or beautiful sight, one lovely sound or delightful scent. Then recall one experience of joy, one of beauty, and another of love.

Remembering love is recalling a state of unity, recognizing a state of consciousness with no separations. Our attention becomes organized and coherent, with no psychic disorder. Self-consciousness disappears when we love; our sense of time becomes an endless now without duration. Love is intrinsically motivated, because we aren't concerned with advancing our own self-interests. It is its own goal.

Loving without an object — being love — is the seminal, transcendent flow experience that Csikszentmihalyi described as determining our quality of life. In flow experiences, action and awareness are merged; people stop being aware of themselves as separate from the actions they are performing. All flow activities — sex, sports, yoga, martial arts, music, the creative arts — stem from loving attention. By remembering love, we experience our true nature as undiluted awareness, and we reveal to ourselves our power to change our minds, and to change our lives.

The purpose of this book is to demonstrate that our minds are joined. As such, any personal transformation can and does have global effects. Just one person experiencing true peace for just one moment affirms our human potential for transformation. A consciousness of unity within any one person radiates out to all. God enters the world through the consciousness of you and me.

Our call to science-minded people to consider that prayer makes sense may seem radical, but as spiritual teacher Marianne Williamson declares, anything short of radical change is an insufficient response to the challenge of our times. Let's try something different. Let's try being still. Let us remember that it is not only what we do, but also what we stop doing that matters. Instead of regretting our past, and fearing our future, let us embrace the present. Along with everything else we are doing to save the world, let's do *nothing*.

The peace process begins in our own minds. "Without peace within, peace in the world is an empty wish," wrote Paul Ferrini. "Like love, peace is extended. It cannot be brought from the world to the heart. It must be brought from each heart to another, and thus to all mankind." [11]

This is the nature and method of our human opportunity. We are the heart of the mind.

Chapter Notes

Introduction

1. Viktor Frankl, *Man's Search for Meaning* (New York: Simon & Schuster, 1959).
2. Albert Einstein, *Out of My Later Years* (Secaucus, N.J.: The Citadel Press, 1956).
3. Armstrong, Karen, *A History of God: The 4000-Year Quest of Judaism Christianity, and Islam* (New York: Alfred A. Knopf, 1993).
4. Ken Wilber, *The Marriage of Sense and Soul: Integrating Science and Religion* (New York: Random House, 1998).
5. Joan Borysenko, *The Ways of the Mystic* (Carlsbad, Calif.: Hay House, Inc., 1997).
6. Ken Wilber, *Quantum Questions: Mystical Writings of the World's Great Physicists* (Boston: Shambhala, 1984).
7. Sri Maharaj Nisargadatta, *I Am That* (Durham, N.C.: The Acorn Press, 1997).
8. Carl Sagan in "Science Finds God," *Newsweek,* July 20, 1998, p. 48.
9. David Bohm and Basel Hiley, *The Undivided Universe* (New York: Routledge, 1993).
10. Gangaji, *You Are That! Volume II* (Boulder, Colo.: Satsang Press, 1995), p. 41.

Chapter One: Make Me One with Everything

1. Carl Sagan, *The Demon-Haunted World: Science As a Candle in the Dark* (New York: Ballantine, 1997), p. 302.
2. Ibid., p. 29.
3. Ibid., p. 28.
4. Ibid., p. 35.

5. Karen Armstrong, *A History of God: The 4000-Year Quest of Judaism, Christianity, and Islam* (New York: Alfred A. Knopf, 1993).

6. Charles T. Tart, *Body Mind Spirit: Exploring the Parapsychology of Spirituality* (Charlottesville, Va.: Hampton Roads, 1997).

7. Sri Maharaj Nisargadatta, *I Am That* (Durham, N.C.: The Acorn Press, 1997).

8. Andrew Harvey, *The Essential Mystics: The Soul's Journey into Truth* (San Francisco: HarperSanFrancisco, 1996).

9. Frances Vaughan, *The Inward Arc* (Boston: Shambhala, 1986).

10. Sogyal Rinpoche, *Tibetan Book of Days* (San Francisco: HarperSanFrancisco, 1997).

11. Ken Wilber and Treya Killam Wilber, *Grace and Grit: Spirituality and Healing in the Death of Treya Killam Wilber* (Boston: Shambhala, 1993).

12. Albert Einstein, *Ideas and Opinions* (New York: Bonanza Books, 1956).

13. Albert Einstein, *Out of My Later Years* (Secaucus, N.J.: The Citadel Press, 1956).

14. Ken Wilber in the foreword to Lex Hixon, *Coming Home* (New York: Jeremy Tarcher/Putnam, 1989), p. viii.

15. Mihaly Csikszentmihaly, *Flow: The Psychology of Optimal Experience* (New York: HarperCollins, 1991).

16. Andrew Cohen, "Knowledge, Power & Enlightenment," *What Is Enlightenment?* Spring/Summer 1997, pp. 14–15.

Chapter Two: Experiencing God Directly

1. Herbert Benson, *Timeless Healing: The Power and Biology of Belief* (New York: Simon & Schuster, 1997).

2. Lex Hixon, *Coming Home* (New York: Jeremy Tarcher/Putnam, 1989), p. xii.

3. Gangaji, *You Are That!* (Boulder, Colo.: Satsang Press, 1995).

4. Mahatera Narada, *The Buddha and His Teachings* (Sri Lanka: Buddhist Publication Society, 1988).

5. Ken Wilber, *Spectrum of Consciousness* (Wheaton, Ill.: Quest Books, 1977).

6. Aldous Huxley, *The Perennial Philosophy* (New York: HarperCollins, 1990).

7. Amit Goswami, *The Self-Aware Universe* (New York: Jeremy Tarcher, 1995).

8. Thich Nhat Hanh, *The Diamond That Cuts Through Illusion: Commentaries on the Prajñaparamita Diamond Sutra* (Berkeley, Calif.: Parallax Press, 1992).

9. Brian Swimme, *The Universe Is a Green Dragon* (Santa Fe, N.M.: Bear & Co., 1984).

10. Mahatera Narada, *The Buddha and His Teachings* (Sri Lanka: Buddhist Publication Society, 1988).

11. Sylvia Boorstein, *It's Easier Than You Think: The Buddhist Way to Happiness* (San Francisco: HarperSanFrancisco, 1992).

12. Jacques Lusseyran, *And There Was Light* (New York: Parabola Books, 1994).

13. Bhagavad Gita, translated by Swami Prabhavananda and Christopher Isherwood (New York: Penguin/Mentor Books, 1954).

14. Paramahansa Yogananda, *The Science of Religion* (Los Angeles: Self-Realization Fellowship, 1984).

15. Elaine Pagels, *Gnostic Gospels* (New York: Vintage Books/Random House, 1979).

16. Ibid.

17. Marvin Meyer, *The Secret Teachings of Jesus: Four Gnostic Gospels* (New York: Vintage Books/Random House, 1984).
18. Lawrence Kushner, *River of Light* (Woodstock, Vt.: Jewish Lights Publishing, 1981).
19. Daniel Matt, *Essential Kabbalah* (San Francisco: HarperSanFrancisco, 1994).
20. Ibid., p. 261.
21. Deepak Chopra, *The Seven Spiritual Laws of Success* (Novato, Calif.: New World Library, 1993).

Chapter Three: The Physics of Miracles

1. H.E. Puthoff and R. Targ, "A Perceptual Channel for Information Transfer over Kilometer Distances: Historical Perspective and Recent Research." *Proc. IEEE* 64, no. 3, (March 1976): pp. 329–254; R. Targ and H.E. Puthoff, "Information Transfer Under Conditions of Sensory Shielding." *Nature* 251 (1975): pp. 602–607; H.E. Puthoff, R. Targ, and E.C. May, "Experimental Psi Research: Implication for Physics," *AAAS Proceedings of the 1979 Symposium on the Role of Consciousness in the Physical World,* 1961.
2. A. Einstein, B. Podolsky, and N. Rosen, "Can a Quantum Mechanical Description of Physical Reality Be Considered Complete?" *Physical Review* 47 (May 15, 1935): pp. 777–780.
3. S. Freedman and J. Clauser, "Experimental Test of Local Hidden Variable Theories," *Physical Review Letters* 28 (1972): pp. 934–941; A. Aspect et al., "Experimental Tests of Bell's Inequalities Using Time-Varying Analyzers," Physical Review Letters 49 (December 20, 1982): pp. 1804–1907; Nicholas Gisin, "Signals Travel Faster than Light," in Malcolm Brown, *The New York Times,* July 22, 1997.
4. S. Dürr, T. Nonn, and G. Rempe, "Origin of Quantum-Mechanical Complementarity Probed by a 'Which-Way' Experiment in an Atom Interferometer," *Nature* 395, no. 3 (September 1998).
5. Brian Josephson, "Biological Utilization of Quantum Nonlocality," *Foundations of Physics* 21 (1991): pp. 197–207.
6. David Bohm and Basel Hiley, *The Undivided Universe* (New York: Routledge, 1993).
7. Russell Targ and Jane Katra, *Miracles of Mind: Exploring Nonlocal Consciousness and Spiritual Healing* (Novato, Calif.: New World Library, 1998).
8. Ken Kress, "Parapsychology in Intelligence: A Personal Review and Conclusions," *Studies in Intelligence* 21, no. 4, (1977); also *Journal of Scientific Exploration* 13 (Spring 1999): pp. 69–87.
9. Joseph McMoneagle, *Mind Trek* (Northfolk, Va.: Hampton Roads, 1993).
10. George Hansen, Marilyn Schlitz, and Charles Tart in Russell Targ and Keith Harary, *The Mind Race* (New York: Villard, 1984), pp. 265-269.
11. Louisa Rhine, "Frequency and Types of Experience in Spontaneous Precognition." *Journal of Parapsychology* 16 (1954): pp. 93–123.
12. S. Freud, "Dreaming and Telepathy," in G. Devereux, (Ed.), *Psychoanalysis and the Occult* (New York: International Universities Press, 1953).
13. Jule Eisenbud, *Parapsychology and the Unconscious* (Berkeley, Calif.: North Atlantic Books, 1986).
14. Montague Ullman and Stanley Krippner with Alan Vaughan, *Dream Telepathy* (New

York: MacMillan Publishing Company, 1973).

15. William Erwin in Montague Ullman and Stanley Krippner with Alan Vaughan, *Dream Telepathy* (New York: MacMillan Publishing Company, 1973).

16. D. Bem and C. Honorton, "Does Psi Exist? Replicable Evidence for an Anomalous Process of Information Transfer," *Psychological Bulletin* (January 1994).

17. Richard Broughton and Cheryl Alexander, "Autoganzfeld II: An Attempted Replication of the PRL Ganzfeld Research," *Journal of Parapsychology* (September 1997): pp. 209–227.

18. Charles Honorton and Diane C. Ferari, "Future-Telling: A Meta-Analysis of Forced-Choice Precognition Experiments," *Journal of Parapsychology* 53 (December 1989): pp. 281–209.

19. R. Targ, J. Katra, D. Brown, and W. Wiegand, "Viewing the Future: A Pilot Study with an Error-Detecting Protocol," *Journal of Scientific Exploration* 9, no. 3 (1995): pp. 367–380.

20. Dean Radin, *The Conscious Universe* (San Francisco: HarperEdge, 1997).

21. Helmut Schmidt and Lee Pantas, "PK Tests with Internally Different Machines," *Journal of Parapsychology* 36 (1972): pp. 222–232.

22. Helmut Schmidt, "Random Generators and Living Systems as Targets in Retro-PK Experiments," *Journal of ASPR* 91 (1997): pp. 1–14.

23. Karlis Osis and Donna McCormick, "Kinetic Effects at the Ostensible Location of an Out-of-Body Projection During Perceptual Testing," *Journal of ASPR* (July 1980): pp. 319–329.

24. Kenneth Ring and Sharon Cooper, "Near-Death and Out-of-Body Experiences in the Blind: A Study of Apparent Eyeless Vision," *Journal of Near Death Studies* (Winter 1997): pp. 101–147.

25. B. J. Dunne, R. G. Jahn, and R. D. Nelson, "Precognitive Remote Perception," Princeton Engineering Anomalies Research Laboratory (Report), August 1983.

26. Ludwig Wittgenstein, *Tractatus-Logico Philosophicus* (New York: Routledge, 1974), p. 147.

27. Ramana Maharshi in *Be As You Are: The Teachings of Sri Ramana Maharshi*, David Godman, ed. (London: Penguin/Arkana, 1985), p. 195.

Chapter Four: What Survives?

1. Leo Tolstoy in Sylvia Cranston and Carey Williams, *Reincarnation: A New Horizon in Science, Religion, and Society* (New York: Julian Press/Crown, 1984).

2. Sylvia Cranston and Carey Williams, *Reincarnation: A New Horizon in Science, Religion, and Society* (New York: Julian Press/Crown, 1984).

3. F.W.H. Myers, in *Human Personality and Its Survival of Bodily Death*, Suzy Smith, ed. (New Hyde Park, N.Y.: University Books, 1961).

4. Ibid., p. 3.

5. D. Scott Rogo, *Parapsychology: A Century of Inquiry* (New York: Taplinger Publishing Company, 1975), p. 259; also *Proceedings of the Society of Psychical Research* 36 (1927): pp. 517–524.

6. Reuters News Service, January 31, 1998.

7. F.W.H. Myers, in *Human Personality and Its Survival of Bodily Death*, Suzy Smith, ed. (New Hyde Park, N.Y.: University Books, 1961).

8. William James in F.W.H. Myers, O. Lodge, W. Leaf, and W. James, "A Record of Observations of Certain Phenomena of Trance" in *Proceedings of the Society for Psychical Research* 6 (1889–90): p. 653.

9. Alan Gauld, *Mediumship and Survival* (London: Paladin/Granada, 1983).

10. Brian Inglis, *Natural and Supernatural* (London: Hodder and Stoughton, 1977), p. 416.

11. Alan Gauld, *Mediumship and Survival* (New York: Paladin/Granada, 1983), pp. 71-73.

12. Bhagavad Gita, translated by Swami Prabhavananda and Christopher Isherwood (New York: Mentor Books, 1954).

13. Buddha, in Sylvia Cranston and Carey Williams, *Reincarnation: A New Horizon in Science, Religion, and Society* (New York: Julian Press/Crown, 1984), p. 255.

14. Ibid., p. 206.

15. Ibid., p. 220.

16. Simcha Raphael, *Jewish Views of the Afterlife* (Northvale, N.J.: Jason Aronson, 1994).

17. Ibid., p. 252.

18. Ibid., p. 334.

19. Ian Stevenson, *Twenty Cases Suggestive of Reincarnation* (New York: American Society for Psychical Research, 1966).

20. Ian Stevenson, *Where Reincarnation and Biology Intersect* (Westport, Conn.: Praeger, 1997).

21. Ian Stevenson, *Children Who Remember Previous Lives* (Charlottesville, Va.: The University Press of Virginia, 1987).

22. Robert Almeder, "A Critique of Arguments Offered Against Reincarnation," *Journal of Scientific Exploration* 11, no. 4 (1997).

23. Robert Almeder, *Death and Personal Survival: The Evidence for Life After Death* (Lanham, Md.: Rowman & Littlefield Publishers, Inc., 1992).

24. Claire Sylvia, *A Change of Heart* (New York: Little Brown & Co., 1997), p. 90.

25. Carl Jung, *Psychological Foundation for Belief in Spirits,* 1910.

26. Rupert Sheldrake in Claire Sylvia, *A Change of Heart* (New York: Little Brown & Co., 1997), p. 230.

27. Ramana Maharshi, *Be As You Are: The Teachings of Sri Ramana Maharshi,* David Godman, ed. (New York: Arkana/Penguin, 1985), p. 197.

Chapter Five: Using Our Mind to Change Our Life

1. Mihaly Csikszentmihaly, *Flow: The Psychology of Optimal Experience* (New York: HarperCollins, 1991), p. 20.

2. Ibid., p. 33.

3. Jon Kabat-Zinn, *Full Catastrophe Living: Using the Wisdom of Your Body and Mind to Face Stress, Pain, and Illness* (New York: Delta Books, 1990); also Jon Kabat-Zinn, "The Contemplative Mind in Society," *Noetic Sciences Review* 35, Autumn 1995, pp. 14–21.

4. Herbert Benson, *Timeless Healing: The Power and Biology of Belief* (New York: Simon & Schuster, 1997), pp. 146–147.

5. Fred Sicher, Elisabeth Targ, Dan Moore, and Helene Smith, "A Randomized Double-Blind Study of the Effect of Distant Healing in a Population with Advanced AIDS," *Western Journal of Medicine* 169 (December 1998): pp. 356–363.

6. Randolph C. Byrd, "Positive Therapeutic Effects of Intercessory Prayer in a Coronary

Care Unit Population," *Southern Medical Journal* 81, no. 7 (July 1988): pp. 826–829.

7. W.G. Braud and M.J. Schlitz, "A Methodology for an Objective Study of Transpersonal Imagery," Journal of Scientific Exploration 3, no. 1 (1989): pp. 43–63; and W. G. Braud and M. J. Schlitz, "Consciousness Interactions with Remote Biological Systems: Anomalous Intentionality Effects," *Subtle Energies* 2, no. 1 (1991): pp. 1–46.

8. W.G. Braud, "Distant Mental Influence of Rate of Hemolysis of Human Red Blood Cells," *JASPR 84*, no. 1 (January 1990): pp. 1–24.

9. Beverly Rubik and Elizabeth Rauscher, "Effects on Motility Behavior and Growth Rate of Salmonella Typhimurium in the Presence of Olga Worrall," in W.G. Roll (ed.), *Research in Parapsychology* 1979 (Metuchen, N.J.: Scarecrow Press, 1980).

10. Anita Watkins and Graham Watkins, "Possible PK Effects on the Resuscitation of Anesthetized Mice," *Journal of Parapsychology* 35 (1971): pp. 257–272.

11. Marilyn Schlitz, "PK on Living Systems: Further Studies with Anesthetized Mice," *Journal of Parapsychology* 46 (1982): pp. 51–52.

12. Marilyn Schlitz and Stephen LaBerge, "Covert Observation Increases Skin Conductance in Subjects Unaware of When They Are Being Observed: A Replication," *Journal of Parapsychology* (September 1997): pp. 185–196.

13. W. Braud and M. Schlitz, "Psychokinetic Influence on Electro-Dermal Activity," *Journal of Parapsychology* 47 (1983): pp. 95–119.

14. Personal communication from Dr. Braud to the authors.

15. Larry Dossey, "Healing Happens," *Utne Reader,* September/October 1995, p. 52–53.

16. Dean Radin, "Where, When, and Who Is the Self" (paper presented at Interval Research Corporation, March 17, 1998).

17. Joel S. Goldsmith, *The Art of Spiritual Healing* (San Francisco: HarperCollins, 1959), p. 73.

18. *A Course in Miracles* (Glen Ellen, Calif.: Foundation for Inner Peace, 1975).

Chapter Six: Why Scientists Pray

1. Roger Walsh, Frances Vaughan, and John Mack, *Paths Beyond Ego: The Transpersonal Vision* (Los Angeles: Jeremy P. Tarcher, 1993), p. 2.

2. Ibid., p. 2.

3. F. Alexander, "Buddhist Training as an Artificial Catatonia (The Biological Meaning of Psychic Occurrences)," *Psychoanalytic Review* 18 (1931): pp. 129–145.

4. Sam Menahem, *When Therapy Isn't Enough: The Healing Power of Prayer & Psychotherapy* (Winfield, Ill.: Relaxed Books, 1997), p. 204.

5. Jacob Needleman, *Lost Christianity* (New York: Doubleday, 1980), p. 60.

6. George Leonard and Michael Murphy, *The Life We Are Given* (New York: Jeremy Tarcher/Putnam, 1995).

7. Roger Walsh, Frances Vaughan, and John Mack, *Paths Beyond Ego: The Transpersonal Vision* (Los Angeles: Jeremy Tarcher, 1993), p. 3.

8. Roger Walsh, "New Views of Timeless Experiences: Contemporary Research on the Nature and Significance of Transpersonal Experience," *The Heffter Review,* 1998.

9. Abraham Maslow, *The Farther Reaches of Human Nature* (New York: Viking Press, 1971); and Abraham Maslow, *Toward a Psychology of Being* (Princeton, N.J.: Van Nostrand Reinhold, 1968), p. iv.

10. William James, *The Varieties of Religious Experience* (New York: Viking/Penguin, 1982), p. 258.

11. Richard Bucke, *Cosmic Consciousness* (New York: E.P. Dutton & Co., 1969), p. 3.

12. Sharon Salzberg, *Loving-Kindness* (Boston: Shambhala, 1997), p. 12.

13. Sri Nisargadatta Maharaj, *I Am That: Talks with Sri Nisargadatta Maharaj,* Sudhakar Dikshit, ed., (Durham, N.C.: The Acorn Press, 1973).

14. Jon Kabat-Zinn, *Wherever You Go There You Are* (New York: Hyperion, 1994), p. 33.

15. Thich Nhat Hanh, *Peace Is Every Step* (New York: Bantam Books, 1991), p. 10.

16. Sharon Salzberg, *Loving-Kindness* (Boston: Shambhala, 1997), p. 1.

17. Thich Nhat Hanh, *Living Buddha, Living Christ* (New York: Riverhead/Putnam, 1995).

18. Ramana Maharshi, "Who Am I?" in *The Collected Works of Ramana Maharshi,* trans. by T. Venkataran (Tiruvannamalai, India: Sri Ramanasramam, 1955).

19. Sri Nisargadatta Maharaj, *I Am That:Talks with Sri Nisargadatta Maharaj,* Sudhakar Dikshit, ed., (Durham, N.C.: The Acorn Press, 1973), p. 8.

20. Dean Brown, *Direct from Sanskrit: New Translations of Seven Upanishads, The Aphorisms of Patanjali, and Other Microcosmic Texts of Ancient India* (Los Angeles: Philosophical Research Society, 1996).

21. Joel Goldsmith, *Consciousness Unfolding* (New York: Citadel Press/Carol Publishing Group, 1994), p. 172.

22. David A. Cooper, *The Heart of Stillness* (New York: Bell Tower/Crown, 1992), p. 63.

23. The Dalai Lama, in Jean-Claude Carriere, "Facing the Future," *New Age Journal,* Nov./Dec. 1995, p. 146.

24. David A. Cooper, *The Heart of Stillness* (New York: Bell Tower/Crown, 1992).

25. Thomas Keating, *Intimacy with God* (New York: Crossroad Publishing, 1994), p. 3; and Thomas Keating, "The Method of Centering Prayer" pamphlet, St. Benedict's Monastery, Colorado, 1995.

26. Thomas Keating, in Cynthia Bourgeault, "From Woundedness to Union," *Gnosis,* 34, Winter 1995, pp. 41–45.

27. Thomas Keating, *Intimacy with God* (New York: Crossroad Publishing, 1994).

28. Thich Nhat Hanh, *Living Buddha, Living Christ* (New York: Riverhead/Putnam, 1995), p. 154.

29. Joseph Bailey, *The Serenity Principle* (San Francisco: HarperSanFrancisco, 1990).

30. *The New York Times,* April 30, 1998.

31. Carl Jung, in "The Bill W.–Carl Jung Letters." *ReVision* 10, no. 2 (1987): pp. 19–21.

32. Ibid.

33. *The New York Times,* December 6, 1997, p. A8.

34. Lewis Lapham, *The Wall Street Journal,* May 13, 1988.

35. Joe Dominguez and Vicki Robin, *Your Money or Your Life* (New York: Penguin Books, 1992), p. 172.

36. Carl Jung, *The Collected Works of C. G. Jung,* Vol. 9, Pt. 1 (Princeton: Princeton Univ. Press, 1969).

37. Georges Van Vrekhem, *Beyond the Human Species: The Life and Work of Sri Aurobindo and the Mother* (St. Paul, Minn.: Paragon House, 1998).

38. Albert Einstein, *Ideas and Opinions* (New York: Bonanza Books, 1956), p. 12.

39. Sir Arthur Eddington in Alan H. Batten, "A Most Rare Vision: Eddington's Thinking

on the Relation Between Science and Religion," *Journal of Scientific Exploration* 9, no. 2 (Summer 1995): pp. 231–234.

40. Joel Goldsmith, *Spiritual Interpretation of Scripture* (Marina del Rey, Calif.: DeVorss & Co., 1947); and Joel Goldsmith, *Consciousness Unfolding* (New York: Citadel Press/Carol Publishing Group, 1994), p. 51.

41. Herbert Benson, *Timeless Healing: The Power and Biology of Belief* (New York: Simon & Schuster, 1997), p. 301.

42. Ernest Wood, *Yoga* (Baltimore, Md.: Penguin, 1962), p. 30.

43. John Blofeld in David Cooper, *The Heart of Stillness* (New York: Bell Tower/Crown, 1992), p. 207.

44. *A Course in Miracles,* (Glen Ellen, Calif.: Foundation for Inner Peace, 1975); and Sri Nisargadatta Maharaj, *I Am That: Talks with Sri Nisargadatta Maharaj,* Sudhakar Dikshit, ed. (Durham, N.C.: The Acorn Press, 1973).

45. Ramana Maharshi in *Be as You Are: The Teachings of Ramana Maharshi,* David Godman, ed. (London: Penguin/Arkana, 1985), p. 88.

46. Nisargadatta, *I Am That,* p. 18.

47. Igor Kungurtsev, "Nonduality and Western Seekers," *Gnosis* 39, Spring 1996, p. 24.

48. Gangaji, *You Are That!* (Novato, Calif.: The Gangaji Foundation, 1996).

49. Igor Kungurtsev, "Nonduality and Western Seekers," *Gnosis* 39, Spring 1996, p. 24.

50. Ibid., p. 22.

Chapter Seven: The Heart of the Mind

1. Paramahansa Yogananda, *The Science of Religion* (Los Angeles, Calif.: Self-Realization Fellowship, 1984).

2. Sylvia Boorstein, *It's Easier Than You Think: The Buddhist Way to Happiness* (San Francisco: HarperSanFrancisco, 1997).

3. Sri Nisargadatta Maharaj, *I Am That: Talks with Sri Nisargadatta Maharaj.* Sudhakar Dikshit, ed. (Durham, N.C.: The Acorn Press, 1973), p. xxii.

4. Gangaji, *You Are That! Vol. I* (Boulder, Colo.: Satsang Press, 1996), p. 165.

5. Gerald Jampolsky, *Love Is Letting Go of Fear* (Berkeley, Calif.: Celestial Arts, 1979); and Gerald Jampolsky and Diane Cirincione, *Change Your Mind, Change Your Life* (New York: Bantam Books, 1994).

6. *A Course in Miracles* (Glen Ellen, Calif.: Foundation for Inner Peace, 1975).

7. Marianne Williamson, "Return to Prayer," *Science of Mind* 69, no. 9 (Sept. 1996): p. 43; also Marianne Williamson, *Illuminata: A Return to Prayer* (New York: Random House, 1994).

8. Ibid.

9. Sylvia Boorstein, *It's Easier Than You Think: The Buddhist Way to Happiness* (San Francisco: HarperSanFrancisco, 1997).

10. Gangaji, *You Are That! Vol. II* (Boulder, Colo.: Satsang Press, 1996), pp. 38, 209.

11. Paul Ferrini, *The 12 Steps of Forgiveness* (South Deerfield, Mass.: Heartways Press, 1997).

Bibliography

Alexander, F. "Buddhist Training as an Artificial Catatonia (The Biological Meaning of Psychic Occurrences)." *Psychoanalytic Review* 18 (1931): pp. 129–145.

Almeder, Robert. *Death and Personal Survival: The Evidence for Life After Death.* Lanham, Md.: Rowman & Littlefield Publishers, 1992.

Almeder, Robert. "A Critique of Arguments Offered Against Reincarnation," *Journal of Scientific Exploration* 11, no. 4, (1997).

Armstrong, Karen. *A History of God: The 4000-Year Quest of Judaism, Christianity, and Islam.* New York: Alfred A. Knopf, 1993.

Aspect, A., et al., "Experimental Tests of Bell's Inequalities Using Time-Varying Analyzers." *Physical Review Letters,* 49 (December 20, 1982): pp. 1804–1907.

Ayer, Alfred. *Language Truth and Logic.* New York: Dover Publications, 1946.

Bailey, Joseph. *The Serenity Principle.* San Francisco: HarperSanFrancisco, 1990.

Bem, D., and C. Honorton. "Does Psi Exist? Replicable Evidence for an Anomalous Process of Information Transfer." *Psychological Bulletin* (January 1994).

Benor, Daniel J. *Healing Research.* Volume 1. Munich, Germany: Helix Verlag, 1992.

Benson, Herbert. *Timeless Healing: The Power and Biology of Belief.* New York: Simon & Schuster, 1997.

Bhagavad Gita. Translated by Swami Prabhavananda and Christopher Isherwood. New York: Penguin/Mentor Books, 1954.

Bohm, David and Basel Hiley. *The Undivided Universe.* New York: Routledge, 1993.

Boorstein, Sylvia. *It's Easier Than You Think: The Buddhist Way to Happiness.* San Francisco: Harper San Francisco, 1997.

Borysenko, Joan. *The Ways of the Mystic.* Carlsbad, Calif.: Hay House, Inc., 1997.

Bourgeault, Cynthia. "From Woundedness to Union." *Gnosis*, no. 34, Winter, (1995): 41–45.

Braud, W.G. "Distant Mental Influence of Rate of Hemolysis of Human Red Blood Cells." *JASPR* 84, no. 1 (January 1990): 1–24.

Braud, W.G., and M.J. Schlitz. "Consciousness Interactions with Remote Biological Systems: Anomalous Intentionality Effects." *Subtle Energies* 2, no. 1 (1991): 1–6.

Braud, W., and M. Schlitz. "Psychokinetic Influence on Electro-Dermal Activity." *Journal of Parapsychology* 47 (1983): 95–119.

Braud, W., D. Shafer, K. McNeill, and V. Guerra. "Attention Focusing Facilitated Through Remote Mental Interaction." *JASPR* 89, no. 2 (April 1995): 113–114.

Broughton, Richard, and Cheryl Alexander. "Autoganzfeld II: An Attempted Replication of the PRL Ganzfeld Research," *Journal of Parapsychology* (September 1997): 209–227.

Brown, Dean. *Direct from Sanskrit: New Translations of Seven Upanishads, the Aphorisms of Patanjali, and Other Microcosmic Texts of Ancient India.* Los Angeles: Philosophical Research Society, 1996.

Bucke, Richard. *Cosmic Consciousness.* New York: E.P. Dutton & Co., 1969.

Byrd, Randolph C. "Positive Therapeutic Effects of Intercessory Prayer in a Coronary Care Unit Population." *Southern Medical Journal* 81, no. 7 (July 1988): 826–829.

Chopra, Deepak. *The Seven Spiritual Laws of Success.* Novato, Calif.: New World Library, 1994.

Cohen, Andrew. "Knowledge, Power & Enlightenment." *What Is Enlightenment?* (Spring/Summer 1997): 14–15.

Cooper, David. *God Is a Verb.* New York: Riverhead Books, 1997.

Cooper, David A. *The Heart of Stillness.* New York: Bell Tower/Crown, 1992.

Cranston, Sylvia, and Carey Williams. *Reincarnation: A New Horizon in Science, Religion, and Society.* New York: Julian Press/Crown, 1984.

Csikszentmihaly, Mihaly. *Flow: The Psychology of Optimal Experience.* New York: HarperCollins, 1991.

Dalai Lama, His Holiness. *The Good Heart.* Boston: Wisdom Publications, 1996.

Diamond, L. Malcolm, and Thomas V. Litzenberg. *The Logic of God.* New York: Bobbs-Merrill, 1975.

Dominguez, Joe, and Vicki Robin. *Your Money or Your Life.* New York: Penguin Books, 1992.

Doore, Gary. *What Survives? Contemporary Explorations of Life After Death.* Los Angeles: Jeremy Tarcher, 1990.

Dossey, Larry. "Healing Happens." *Utne Reader,* September/October 1995, pp. 52–59.

Dossey, Larry. *Meaning & Medicine: Lessons from a Doctor's Tales of Breakthrough and Healing.* New York: Bantam Books, 1992.

Dunne, B.J., R.G. Jahn, and R.D. Nelson. "Precognitive Remote Perception," Princeton Engineering Anomalies Research Laboratory (Report) August 1983.

Dürr, S., T. Nonn, and G. Rempe. "Origin of Quantum-Mechanical Complementarity Probed by a 'Which-Way' Experiment in an Atom Interferometer." *Nature* 395, no. 3 (September 1998).

Eddington, Sir Arthur, in Alan H. Batten. "A Most Rare Vision: Eddington's Thinking on the Relation Between Science and Religion." *Journal of Scientific Exploration* 9, no. 2

(Summer 1995): 231–234.

Einstein, Albert. *Ideas and Opinions.* New York: Bonanza Books, 1956.

Einstein, Albert. *Out of My Later Years.* Secaucus, N.J.: The Citadel Press, 1956.

Einstein, A., B. Podolsky, and N. Rosen. "Can a Quantum Mechanical Description of Physical Reality Be Considered Complete?" *Physical Review* 47 (May 15, 1935): 777–780.

Eisenbud, Jule. *Parapsychology and the Unconscious.* Berkeley, Calif.: North Atlantic Books, 1986.

Ferrini, Paul. *The 12 Steps of Forgiveness.* South Deerfield, Mass.: Heartways Press, 1997.

Foundation for Inner Peace. *A Course In Miracles.* Glen Ellen, Calif.: Foundation for Inner Peace, 1975.

Freud, S. "Dreaming and Telepathy." In G. Devereux, (ed.), *Psychoanalysis and the Occult.* New York: International Universities Press, 1953.

Frankl, Viktor. *Man's Search for Meaning.* New York: Simon & Schuster, 1959.

Freedman, S. and J. Clauser. "Experimental Test of Local Hidden Variable Theories." *Physical Review Letters* 28 (1972): 934–941.

Gangaji. *You Are That!,* Volumes I & II. Boulder, Colorado: Satsang Press, 1995.

Gauld, Alan. *Mediumship and Survival.* London: Paladin/Granada, 1983.

Goldsmith, Joel. *Spiritual Interpretation of Scripture.* Marina del Rey, Calif.: DeVorss & Co., 1947.

Goldsmith, Joel. *Consciousness Unfolding.* New York: Citadel Press/Carol Publishing, 1994.

Goswami, Amit. *The Self-Aware Universe,* New York: Jeremy Tarcher, 1995.

Grosso, Michael, in Charles T. Tart. *Body Mind Spirit: Exploring the Parapsychology of Spirituality.* Charlottesville, Va.: Hampton Roads, 1997.

Hanh, Thich Nhat. *The Diamond That Cuts Through Illusion: Commentaries on the Prajñaparamita Diamond Sutra,* Berkeley, Calif.: Paralax Press, 1992.

Hanh, Thich Nhat. *Living Buddha, Living Christ.* New York: Riverhead/Putnam, 1995.

Hanh, Thich Nhat. *Peace Is Every Step.* New York: Bantam Books, 1991.

Harvey, Andrew. *The Essential Mystics: The Soul's Journey into Truth.* San Francisco: HarperSanFrancisco, 1996.

Hixon, Lex. *Coming Home: The Experience of Enlightenment in Sacred Traditions.* New York: Jeremy Tarcher, 1989.

Holy Bible, King James Version.

Honorton, Charles and Ferari, Diane C. "Future-Telling: A Meta-Analysis of Forced-Choice Precognition Experiments." *Journal of Parapsychology* 53 (December 1989): 281–209.

Huxley, Aldous. *The Perennial Philosophy.* New York: HarperCollins, 1990.

James, William. *The Varieties of Religious Experience.* New York: Viking/Penguin, 1982.

Jampolsky, Gerald. *Love Is Letting Go of Fear.* Berkeley, Calif.: Celestial Arts, 1979.

Jampolsky, Gerald, and Diane Cirincione. *Change Your Mind, Change Your Life.* New York: Bantam Books, 1994.

Josephson, Brian. "Biological Utilization of Quantum Nonlocality." *Foundations of Physics* 21 (1991): 197–207.

Jung, Carl. *The Collected Works of C.G. Jung, Vol. 9, Part. 1.* Princeton: Princeton Univ. Press, 1969.

Kabat-Zinn, Jon. *Full Catastrophe Living: Using the Wisdom of Your Body and Mind to Face Stress, Pain, and Illness.* New York: Delta Books, 1990.

Kabat-Zinn, Jon. *Wherever You Go There You Are.* New York: Hyperion, 1994.

Kabat-Zinn, Jon. "The Contemplative Mind in Society." *Noetic Sciences Review* 35 (Autumn 1995): 14–21.

Kamenetz, Rodger. *The Jew and the Lotus.* San Francisco: HarperSanFrancisco, 1994.

Keating, Thomas. *Intimacy with God.* New York: Crossroad Publishing, 1994.

Kress, Ken. "Parapsychology in Intelligence: A Personal Review and Conclusions." *Studies in Intelligence* 21, no. 4 (1977).

Krishnamurti, J. *Think On These Things.* New York: Harper & Row, 1970.

Kushner, Lawrence. *The River of Light.* Woodstock, Vt.: Jewish Lights Publishing, 1981.

Leonard, George and Michael Murphy. *The Life We Are Given.* New York: Tarcher/ Putnam, 1995.

Lusseyran, Jacques. *And There Was Light.* New York: Parabola Books, 1994.

Maharshi, Ramana. *The Spiritual Teachings of Ramana Maharshi.* Boston: Shambhala, 1988.

Maharshi, Ramana. *Be As You Are: The Teachings of Sri Ramana Maharshi,* David Godman, ed. New York: Arkana/Penguin, 1985.

Maharshi, Ramana. *The Teachings of Bhagavan Sri Ramana Maharshi in His Own Words,* Arthur Osborne, ed. London: Rider & Co., 1962.

Maharshi, Ramana. *Talks With Sri Ramana Maharshi.* Tiruvannamalaj, India: Sri Ramanasramam, 1955.

Maharshi, Ramana. "Who Am I?" in *The Collected Works of Ramana Maharshi,* trans. by T. Venkataran. Tiruvannamalai, India: Sri Ramanasramam, 1955.

Maslow, Abraham. *The Farther Reaches of Human Nature.* New York: Viking Press, 1971.

Maslow, Abraham. *Toward a Psychology of Being.* Princeton, N.J.: Van Nostrand Reinhold, 1968.

Matt, Daniel. *Essential Kabbalah.* San Francisco: HarperSanFrancisco, 1994.

McMoneagle, Joseph. *Mind Trek.* Norfolk, Va.: Hampton Roads Publishing, 1993.

Menahem, Sam. *When Therapy Isn't Enough: The Healing Power of Prayer & Psychotherapy.* Winfield, Ill.: Relaxed Books, 1997.

Meyer, Marvin. *The Secret Teachings of Jesus: Four Gnostic Gospels.* New York: Vintage Books/Random House, 1984.

Mitchell, Stephen. *The Gospel According to Jesus.* New York: HarperCollins, 1991.

Monroe, Robert. *Journeys Out of the Body.* New York: Main Street Books, 1973.

Murphy, Michael. *The Future of the Body.* Los Angeles: Jeremy P. Tarcher, 1992.

Myers, F.W.H. *Human Personality and Its Survival of Bodily Death.* ed. Suzi Smith. Hyde Park, N.Y.: University Books, 1961.

Nagarjuna, philosophy of, in Hayes, Richard P., "Nagarjuna's Appeal." *Journal of Indian Philosophy* (1994): 299–378.

Narada, Mahatera. *The Buddha and His Teachings.* Sri Lanka: Buddhist Publication Society, 1988.

Needleman, Jacob. *Lost Christianity.* New York: Doubleday, 1980.

Nisargadatta Maharaj, Sri. *I Am That: Talks with Sri Nisargadatta Maharaj.* ed. Sudhakar

Dikshit. Durham, N.C.: The Acorn Press, 1977.

Osis, Karlis and Donna McCormick. "Kinetic Effects at the Ostensible Location of an Out-of-Body Projection During Perceptual Testing." *Journal of ASPR* (July 1980): 319–329.

Pagels, Elaine. *Gnostic Gospels*. New York: Vintage Books/Random House, 1979.

Patanjali. Sutras. Swami Prabhavananda and Christopher Isherwood, trans., *How to Know God*. Hollywood, Calif.: Vedanta Press, 1983.

Patanjali. *Effortless Being: The Yoga Sutras of Patanjali*. P. Shearer, trans. London: Unwin, 1989.

Percy, Walker. *Lost in the Cosmos*. New York: Noonday/Farrar, Strauss & Giroux, 1983.

Percy, Walker. *The Message in the Bottle*. New York: Noonday/Farrar, Strauss & Giroux, 1975.

Pierce, Charles S. "A Neglected Argument for the Reality of God," in *Selected Writings,* Philip Wiener, ed. New York: Dover Publications, 1980; Boston: Shambhala, 1988.

Poonja, H.W.L. *Wake Up and Roar,* Eli Jaxon-Bear, ed. Boulder, Colo.: Satsang Press, 1993.

Puthoff, H.E. and R. Targ. "A Perceptual Channel for Information Transfer over Kilometer Distances: Historical Perspective and Recent Research." *Proc. IEEE* 64, no. 3 (March 1976): 329–254.

Puthoff, H.E., R. Targ, and E.C. May. "Experimental Psi Research: Implication for Physics," in the *AAAS Proceedings* of the 1979 Symposium on the Role of Consciousness in the Physical World, (1961).

Radin, Dean. *The Conscious Universe*. San Francisco, Calif.: HarperEdge, 1997.

Ram Dass. *Be Here Now.* New York: Harmony Books, 1971.

Raphael, Simcha. *Jewish Views of the Afterlife*. Northwale, N.J.: Jason Aronson, 1994.

Rhine, Louisa. "Frequency and Types of Experience in Spontaneous Precognition." *Journal of Parapsychology* 16 (1954): 93–123.

Ring, Kenneth, and Sharon Cooper. "Near-Death and Out-of-Body Experiences in the Blind: A Study of Apparent Eyeless Vision." *Journal of Near Death Studies* (Winter 1997): 101–147.

Rinpoche, Sogyal. *Tibetan Book of Days*. San Francisco: HarperSanFrancisco, 1997.

Sagan, Carl. *The Demon-Haunted World: Science As a Candle in the Dark*. New York: Ballantine, 1997.

Salzberg, Sharon. *Loving-Kindness*. Boston: Shambhala, 1997.

Schlitz, Marilyn, and Stephen LaBerge. "Covert Observation Increases Skin Conductance in Subjects Unaware of When They are Being Observed: A Replication." *Journal of Parapsychology* (September 1997): 185–196.

Schmidt, Helmut, and Lee Pantas. "PK Tests with Internally Different Machines." *Journal of Parapsychology* 36 (1972): 222–232.

Schmidt, Helmut. "Random Generators and Living Systems as Targets in Retro-PK Experiments." *Journal of ASPR* 91 (1997): 1–14.

Shearer, P., trans. *Effortless Being: The Yoga Sutras of Patanjali*. London: Unwin, 1989.

St. John of the Cross. *The Dark Night of the Soul*. New York: Image Books/Doubleday, 1990.

Stevenson, Ian. *Children Who Remember Previous Lives*. Charlottesville, Va.: The University Press of Virginia, 1987.

Stevenson, Ian. *Twenty Cases Suggestive of Reincarnation*. New York: American Society for Psychical Research, 1966.

Stevenson, Ian. *Where Reincarnation and Biology Intersect.* Westport, Conn.: Praeger, 1997.

Swimme, Brian. *The Universe Is a Green Dragon.* Santa Fe, N.M.: Bear & Co., 1984.

Sylvia, Claire. *A Change of Heart.* New York: Little Brown & Co., 1997.

Targ, R., and K. Harary. *The Mind Race: Understanding and Using Psychic Abilities.* New York: Villard, 1984.

Targ, Russell, and Jane Katra. *Miracles of Mind: Exploring Nonlocal Consciousness and Spiritual Healing.* Novato, Calif.: New World Library, 1998.

Targ, R. and H. Puthoff. "Information Transfer under Conditions of Sensory Shielding." *Nature,* 251, (1975): 602–607.

Targ, R., J. Katra, D. Brown, and W. Wiegand. "Viewing the Future: A Pilot Study with an Error-Detecting Protocol." *Journal of Scientific Exploration* 9 no. 3 (1995): 67–80.

Tart, Charles T., ed. *Body Mind Spirit: Exploring the Parapsychology of Spirituality.* Charlottesville, Va.: Hampton Roads, 1997.

Tart, Charles T. *States of Consciousness.* New York: E.P. Dutton, 1975.

Tart, Charles T. *Transpersonal Psychologies.* New York: Harper & Row, 1975.

Tart, Charles T. *Waking Up: Overcoming the Obstacles to Human Potential.* Boston: New Science Library/Shambhala, 1986.

Teresa of Avila, Saint. *The Life of Saint Teresa.* Trans. by J.M. Cohen. New York: Penguin Books, 1957.

Twist, Lynn. "The Soul of Money." *Noetic Sciences Review* (Fall 1997): 22–25.

Ullman, Montague, and Stanley Krippner, with Alan Vaughan. *Dream Telepathy.* New York: MacMillan, 1973.

Vaughan, Frances. *The Inward Arc.* Boston: Shambhala, 1986.

Walsh, Roger, Frances Vaughan, and John Mack. *Paths Beyond Ego: The Transpersonal Vision* (A New Consciousness Reader). Los Angeles: Jeremy P. Tarcher, 1993.

Weil, Andrew. *The Natural Mind.* Boston: Houghton Mifflin, 1972.

Wilber, Ken. *Quantum Questions: Mystical Writings of the World's Great Physicists.* Boston: Shambhala, 1984.

Wilber, Ken. *Spectrum of Consciousness.* Wheaton, Ill.: Quest Books, 1977.

Wilber, Ken. *The Atman Project: A Transpersonal View of Human Development.* Wheaton, Ill.: Quest Books, 1996.

Wilber, Ken. *The Marriage of Sense and Soul: Integrating Science and Religion.* New York: Random House, 1998.

Wilber, Ken, and Treya Killam Wilber. *Grace and Grit: Spirituality and Healing in the Life and Death of Treya Killam Wilber.* Boston: Shambhala, 1993.

Williamson, Marianne. *Illuminata: A Return to Prayer.* Marina del Rey, Calif.: DeVorss & Co., 1996.

Williamson, Marianne. "Return to Prayer," in *Science of Mind* 69, no. 9 (Sept. 1996): 40–51.

Wittgenstein, Ludwig. *On Certainty.* New York: HarperCollins, 1986.

Wood, Ernest, *Yoga.* Baltimore, Md.: Penguin, 1962.

Yogananda, Paramahansa. *The Science of Religion.* Los Angeles, Calif.: Self-Realization Fellowship, 1984.

Index